You'll Never Believe It

D0107590

You'll Never Believe It

Retired Lieut.
Anthony Victor Naturale (Natch)

To order additional copies of this book, contact:
Xlibris Corporation
1-888-795-4274
www.Xlibris.com
Orders@Xlibris.com
23265

CONTENTS

DEDICATION

TO MY WIFE,
MADELINE,
MY GUIDING LIGHT
ON THIS JOURNEY;
IN LOVING MEMORY
OF MY PARENTS,
VICTOR AND JOSEPHINE NATURALE;
AND MY SISTER,
"MADIE"

ABOUT THE AUTHOR

FIRST-TIME AUTHOR RETIRED Lieutenant Anthony Naturale's unique perspective and ever-present understated humor brings an edginess to his portrayal of "the cop on the beat" in his nonfiction biography, *You'll Never Believe It.*

What would you do if, out of the blue, you read a book by the first Internal Affairs Commander in the annals of the Township of Montclair, who brought an honest, unflinching exploration of moments you saw from the outside looking in?

Ret. Lt. Anthony Naturale sees no reason why he can't talk about the essence of his life which is scissored with characters from the town he grew up in, went to school with, played football with and chose to protect.

After thirty-four years of guarding the citizens of his hometown, he gives it up and shares. At last you get a chance to really know "Tough Tony." Natch's marvelous sense of humor peppers factual events into a more than good ride and evokes the essence of what it is to be a police officer while, at the same time, giving you an inside but contemporary view of "Old Montclair" through the eyes of a rookie who climbed the ladder in the hierarchy of the "Men in Blue."

Tautly written as only a true storyteller can, and endowed

with a tongue-in-cheek, ironic spin, *You'll Never Believe It* plunges us into the havoc that lies just outside our bedroom windows. Although Tony takes you into the streets and behind the scenes, you always feel the force of what the Police Department does best.

Anthony Naturale resides in Wharton, New Jersey with his wife, Madeline; they have three children and six grandchildren, with number seven arriving very soon.

Naturale continues to be very physically active in bowling, hardball and softball, participating in the last four Senior Olympics as well as playing hardball in a tournament in Cooperstown, New York at the famous Doubleday Hall of Fame Field this fall.

At present Tony is writing *Fitness for Seniors*, with humor, as well as compiling research for a serious novel.

OVERTURE

By Grange Rutan Habermann

PERHAPS I'M CRAZY to even be introducing you to the author of *You'll Never Believe It*—Retired Lieutenant Anthony Naturale of the Montclair Police Department in the State of New Jersey—because I am a "wanna-be Italian."

Reader, consider yourself grabbed. As the author's agent, I have an inside view and you're off to a marvelous party and "who says you have to be Italian?"

Mine was the only 'WASP' family growing up on Oxford Street in Montclair. But there was always the "Italian Connection": my great-grandfather, Frederick Simion Goodman, was one of the original founders and Secretary of the American Waldensian Society at Central Presbyterian Church, which was a place of worship for Italian Catholics who wanted to be Presbyterians in Montclair, New Jersey.

Tony was from Upper Montclair, grew up on Grove Street, adjacent to the Little Italy of Wildwood Avenue, and baptized himself as a "Medi-Italian" . . . a word out of his private clever, quirky and always humorous dictionary.

I present my credentials as I introduce you to the cop

who indulged in nonstop verbal and mental gymnastics as he laid his life on the line . . . and lived to tell about it.

My neighbors were the Campanalongos, the Clements, the Litwins, the DeRosas, the DeStefanos, the Edwins, the Ferlantis, the Galasciones, the Gerardis, the Hollanders, the Quadrels, the Lombardis, the Masceras, the Naspos, the Reccias, the Russos, the Swensons, and Walter Sperling, M.D. It's amazing how many of my neighbors I can remember.

I was exposed to some of the finest Italian gourmet cooking before I even knew it. Everything special and wonderful seemed to end in a vowel. Our celebrated Montclair High School football team had two legendary athletic coaches: Clary Anderson (also a Montclair High graduate, Class of 1930) and Angelo "Butch" Fortunato, a graduate of Fordham University (who played football under the astute and heroic tutelage of the infamous Vince Lombardi, and was one of his original "seven blocks of granite").

Why, even the brook that flowed through our town was named after a guy by the name of "Tony."

I can tell you all my friends' mothers exposed me to sauce. And I knew something was wrong in my house when I asked my mother to make me "pasta and sauce" and she said, "What does it look like?" I told her red with noodles. The next day I sat down to Mueller's elbow macaroni and Campbell's tomato soup.

Over the years, I became good friends with Italians living in Upper Montclair as well in my neighborhood. But there was one woman's friendship I have treasured a lifetime: Mrs. Josephine Naturale, who to this day I privately consider my mother-in-law. She invited me to enter into that sacred and most hallowed part of her kitchen where she prepared her secret recipe for "sauce," AKA "gravy"—which she handed down to her daughter, "Madie," and she had learned from her mother, Grandma Carolina. She actually allowed me to write it down on paper.

I was allowed to ask questions like, "Why are you putting

chunks of Romano cheese in the gravy?" or "Why are you sprinkling in all that wheat germ and not using oregano?"

She shared with me (she felt sorry for me), a direct descendent of Revolutionary War Patriot Ethan Allen of the Green Mountain Boys of Fort Ticonderoga, who fought against the New Yorkers for Vermont, for himself and General Israel Putnam, a leader at the Battle of Bunker Hill, who supposedly gave the command, "Men, you are all marksmen: don't one of you fire until you see the whites of their eyes." (Gen. William Prescott is credited with giving a similar command.) This connection allowed me to become eligible not only to join the Daughters of the American Revolution but the Colonial Dames as well.

So, thanks to all these credentials, and Mrs. Naturale's authentic recipe, I dared, the 'wanna-be Italian,' to enter the *Star-Ledger's* crazy idea to find out who made the best sauce in the State of New Jersey contest. Out of the 285 recipes, sent in by 179 females and 106 males (over 160 called it "sauce" and 125 called it "gravy") . . . on Wednesday, May 9, 2001, the paper announced I won First Honorable Mention with "Gravy for Tony."

When Robbie Naturale and his brothers affectionately gave their grandma the sobriquet "Meatball Gram," I went completely ballistic, because in my mind, she was truly the "Cappa di tutti en la cuccina."

As Historian for Montclair High School's Class of 1956, ironically, and belatedly, it was suggested at one of our meetings for our forty-sixth reunion, by Etta DeNicola Sherry, "Grange, you are simply a misplaced WASP." And all in attendance agreed.

Interestingly enough, another good friend and former classmate, Retired Chief Thomas J. Russo of the Montclair Police Department, introduced me, while a mere sophomore (who only knew of egg salad, watercress, and peanut butter and jelly sandwiches), to something marvelously mysterious by the name of "gobagool."

While the mother of the First Head of Internal Affairs of the Montclair Police Department, Retired Lieutenant Anthony V. Naturale, introduced me not only to "sauce" but "pasta fazool," cream puffs and my very first piece of pizza, in my house treats were for company, and early on I knew I was deprived.

There's more to establish my credentials of knowing the author. In 1955, Fate had me sitting in the living room at 427 Grove Street when Tony brought home his lovely blue-eyed and obviously not Italian bride-to-be: Madeline Tobin. A moment, by the way, which created havoc as we all were instructed to sit properly and wait for the arrival of the firstborn son, just out of the United States Navy, and his sweetheart.

Even though a freshman at Centenary College in Hackettstown, I was given permission, and allowed to leave the campus, to be chauffeured down to the gala of Tony and Madeline's wedding on November 10, 1956, at The Well in Caldwell and just happened to catch the bridal bouquet.

Consequently, I feel qualified, not only as a professional writer and agent, to say a few words (I almost married Tony's brother, Victor, Jr.), but as a family friend of over fifty years, to introduce you to the author.

When Tony retired, the news never made the front pages of newspapers all over the world. There were no extra editions, followed with special supplements, lauding the honest cop who, for thirty-four years, woke up every day; put on his badge and gun, kissed his wife and family good-bye (never knowing if he would return), to drive, early or late at night, through our great town; patrolling the dark streets of the Fourth Ward, downtown, uptown, cruising Bloomfield Avenue and all over town, always ready, never tiring or becoming impatient, to absorb, sponge up and digest the invisible, throbbing, nocturnal pulse beat of the sleeping citizens he took an oath to protect and keep safe from crime: "My Montclair."

It is not so difficult to remember why Naturale matters to so many people, and why he continues to matter. Being a cop was the engine of his life. Tony is one of those unique individuals who brought to his job the value of honesty twenty-four hours a day and seven days a week; he wore it like a badge even when not in uniform. He was formed by an America long gone: born of Italian-American parents who left the City of Newark, passed through the Depression and war into the uncertain realities of peace to raise a family with old-fashioned values.

You'll Never Believe It is about the accomplishments of Tony Naturale and why he matters. You be the judge. He says he is not a writer but a story-teller, and that he is. At one point he wanted me to help him write his autobiography; it never happened, because he did it himself. But in the course of discussing his life, he talked about himself in ways that still had an element of wonder to him. Part of him still cannot believe he has been so lucky to survive so much. More than anything, he loves his family deeply and, through this book, they will see just who their father is and his legacy to them. Tony is wonderful with all children; he is funny and although sometimes called "Tough Tony," I have never seen the tough guy of the legend (although I'm sure many a criminal trembled when arrested). But he never shows that side of himself. I always know I am in the company of an intelligent man, a true gallant, sports lover and leader of men.

The stern, street-smart, savvy, college-educated professional, the "Medi-Italian" has the last laugh. And so will you.

By Father Frank Burla, Immaculate Conception
Church, Montclair, NJ

Whenever I think of Tony Naturale I see his warm, perpetual smile. His son, Steven—we call him "Natch"—is the same way. When he was a student at Immaculate Conception, he too, like his father, was wearing that great open smile.

There are many incidents I could share, but one moment in time stands out, for it typifies not only the kind of police officer Tony was when he was on Montclair's Police Department, but what a truly dedicated and caring man he is to this day.

Some poor kid had just been caught shoplifting; I really cannot remember the crime. Upon arrival at the police station, the kid was so upset because he lost his hat. Before you know it, there goes Tony: leaves the precinct, goes several blocks to look for the lost hat at the scene of the crime, which he found and returned to the boy.

To me, that compassionate act showed the true substance of the man Tony is, for he saw this kid as a human being and not as a criminal.

Madeline Tobin Naturale, Tony's wife

Where did all those good and bad times go? It seems as if it were only yesterday when my handsome "Rookie" would pick me up after work at the Montclair Trust Company Bank on Bloomfield Avenue in beautiful downtown "Old Montclair." Anthony was always there for me, even on the force and all those hours away when he did electrical work— he was always available. Only once, in his entire career, did I not want to bother him on the job.

I vividly remember, even to this day, a Sunday on our way to Immaculate Conception Church when Steven, LeeAnn, Carolyn and I walked out the door of our home on Gordonhurst Avenue and saw a large kitchen knife stuck in the middle of our front door right next to the glass windowpane. At the time I really did not give it much thought, although I wondered how it got there. At Mass I mentioned this knife to my friend Marie and she became extremely agitated and said, "Madeline, that's the sign of the Mafia!"

My mind would not rest and we immediately left church. Anthony was working the eight to four tour, so I called my dad and he immediately came over. He instructed me to call my husband, which I did. Barely minutes later I could hear the siren of his police car as he pulled into the driveway and came running into the house. Anthony never did explain about the knife to me until many years later.

At a very sad moment in my life, when we lost our first child, my husband's wonderful sense of humor came to my rescue. When Dr. Wong came to the house, upon his arrival, he placed his derby hat on the foot of my bed. Wanting to be close, Anthony came to join us and very casually sat at the end of the bed, totally unaware that he had just flattened and ruined the derby. Consequently, a very critical moment suddenly became humorous as Anthony and I started laughing. However, this was not funny to the good doctor as he ranted off a tirade in Chinese at the ruination of his hat.

When I had my last miscarriage Anthony had been on the force barely seven years and we had our three children. We were a happy Catholic family, looking into the future. My call to the precinct was desperate. Anthony told Lieutenant Dempsy, "My wife is bleeding, she's suffering a miscarriage . . . I have to go home right away!"

Totally not in touch with our plight, the Lieutenant said, "You're not going anywhere, my boy, until you are properly relieved."

Anthony told me he marched right by the Lieutenant, grabbed a set of keys to one of the radio cars in the lot and said, "The hell with you . . . my wife is losing our baby! I'm going; you're relieving me. I have to go home and you do what you have to do!"

(This behavior could have cost him his job, and to me Anthony was courageous.)

Over the forty-seven years of our marriage, Anthony has worn many hats . . . and so have I. We've been a marvelous team through our great love for children—all children. Of course, he loved our children but his outreach was mighty and he never tired of connecting to the lost juvenile delinquents and even bringing them home—as well as their friends. For many years I worked for the Board of Education and it seemed our extended youthful family members grew through leaps and bounds. Anthony always found time to fool around or talk seriously, if necessary, and never ignored their need for a word of advice or just a listening ear. There were times when I said to myself, "This can't be my husband! Surely he is a Man of the Cloth!" Thank heavens he was smitten with me and I would see that special look in his eyes. We married young, and the rest is history.

By Steven Naturale, Tony's son

There are so many things about my dad I would like to share, but three thoughts come to the fore.

As I grew up, I saw how my father always treated everyone the same—no matter who they were—with respect and dignity and I, in turn, will always respect him for the values he taught us.

While playing football throughout Immaculate Conception High School and my alma mater, Ramapo State College, no matter where we were playing, rain or shine, from the field I would see my dad up there in the stands, always giving support. Win or lose, he was the first person I would see after the game. He would always give me an honest and straightforward opinion of how he thought I played. Today I realize how much those moments meant to me at the time, and also how lucky I was to share those moments with him.

Whenever I see Dad with my daughter Eve I am amazed! She is so much like him it is scary. They are both entertainers . . . to any audience available. She dances very similar to his crazy style and loves "Poppy" so much. It makes me very happy, as a father, for my daughter to have that type of connection with my father.

By LeeAnn Marie (Naturale) Hurley,
Tony's daughter

There are many things in this book that I never knew about my father when I was growing up. One thing I did know, however, was that he was an extraordinary man. I remember one time when I was young, he and I were walking along Bloomfield Avenue in Montclair when a very tall, lanky black man with an overgrown afro approached us. He greeted my father with a big hug and shook hands vigorously. He acknowledged me and then told my father how happy he was to see him; they stood talking and laughing for a little while. When he walked away, I asked who he was. My father just shrugged and casually said, "He's just some guy I arrested for burglary about a year ago." He had gotten out of prison and was grateful to my father for helping him find a job.

My father's humor and good nature have always allowed him to see the best in everyone. Most people love him because he treats them with a genuine kindness and esteem. It does not matter if that person is the chief of police or a common criminal. I think the criminals especially saw that he responded differently to them than most of the other policemen. Although he could be quite tough, his compassion was ever-present and they respected that about him. This is why, I believe, so many of them were always happy to see him when they got out of jail. They genuinely liked him! Over the years, many people have told me what a great man my father is. This is one thing, however, that I have always known about him!

This book has been trying to break out of him for a very long time. Since I was a child, my father has talked about writing it. Although filled with many funny episodes that have happened to him over the years, *and there have been many,* I believe this book will reveal what a truly unique and kindhearted man he has been all of his life.

I will always love him and I wish him the best of luck with his book. And Dad—*I can't believe* it's finally done!!!

By Carolyn (Naturale) Hughes, Tony's daughter

My father is an extremely kind, honest, caring and generous man with an incredible sense of humor. As long as I can remember he said, "One day I am going to write a book," and of course I always believed he would, for his stories, over the years, have made so many people laugh. You can hear them over and over. I can honestly say they are still funny to this day.

So many times I have been told by various people the wonderful stories of how my dad helped them throughout the years.

But most of all, I can say that I am so proud to be his daughter and could not have asked for a more special and wonderful person to be my dad! I am very blessed.

By Richard Michael Tobin, Tony's nephew

If I told you about my Uncle Tony, "you would not believe it" is truly this man's life!

No one else could have done or had the things that happened in his life occur and still be here on this earth to tell about it!

By Emily Madeline Hurley,
Tony's granddaughter, age 10

I interviewed my grandfather, Tony Naturale. He was born in Orange, New Jersey. He was stationed in Norfolk, Virginia during the Korean War. He was a seaman and then a third-class petty officer. He had many jobs: for example, Oil King and Shore Patrol. He got to see the world, and being in the war helped him to become a police officer. His life was enriched because he was more aware and met a lot of people. I learned more about my grandfather and the Navy. I enjoyed interviewing him because I got to know him better. I am very proud of my grandfather because he served our country.

By Donald Stake, Tony's friend and Best Man

When I think back, I have known Tony Naturale fifty-nine years . . . that's more than a lifetime—we are there!

As a fellow classmate from Mount Hebron to Montclair High School, my good buddy Tony was the class clown; I was very shy and fell back into the crowd.

After school I used to go looking for Tony at 301 Bloomfield Avenue at his father's cleaning business: Ace Cleaners. Whenever Vic Sr. saw me he'd warmly greet me with, "Hey, Don!" Many an hour was spent kibitzing. We really got along great and I always felt welcome . . . even if I couldn't find Tony.

I was best man at his wedding, and then there were all those "lost" years when we both worked two jobs bringing up our kids. By the way, Tony became the "Godfather" to my twin girls, Sharon and Bonnie.

When Tony joined the force, overnight the jokester disappeared and he became one of the finest and most respected police officers Montclair has ever known.

Life gets in the way, as it often does, but to this day, we're connected; Tony's telephone number is Number One on my cell phone.

By William Sweeney, Tony's friend

Tony is not your everyday cop—he is extra-ordinary and

has developed a "Godly" attitude: strong but sensitive towards the needs of others; not always ready to call you out on a wrong move . . . such as a police officer, fireman, government or military authority . . . fixes problems with the least sweat and blood spilt. An authority has to be a role model or do the civil servant's job. You have to make split-second decisions, be in shape of mind, body and spirit; that's Tony Naturale: a great sports lover and Olympian even after his retirement.

By John Healy, Tony's friend

Growing up during the Depression, early on I respected my policeman father, who was a widower and single parent.

Sadly, my mother, Pauline Healy, died of appendicitis at the all-too-young age of twenty-nine, leaving my father, Maurice Healy, the sole responsibility of raising six young boys.

All of us proudly enlisted to serve our country: Maurice, Jr., the United States Air Force; Joseph, the United States Coast Guard; Alvah, the United States Marines; Thomas and Richard were not separated and were in the invasion of Guadacanal; John (that's me) served in the Pacific and Okinawa; Gerard served in the United States Navy on the U.S.S. New Jersey battleship; even my dad, at forty-eight years of age, enlisted in the United States Marines, which was unheard of except in the movies. We had no mother or grandmother to petition a state senator, local parish priest or the President to keep our family safe. I think back and it is unbelievable we all came home to each other.

I met Tony Naturale when I played ball at the Senior Olympics in Florida; he came with a New Jersey team, and the Delaware team was short a player so I went with them. I can only imagine how great Tony must have been as a youngster from Upper Montclair, New Jersey, when he played football for the legendary Clary Anderson and Butch Fortunato. Tony is a born leader in a quiet, aggressive way and we got along well, especially when he was the pitcher and I was the catcher; he is a southpaw and would set up his sweeping curveball that would come in on the outside and drop inside for a strike. As our captain we all looked up to him, always cheering us on, keeping score and making it happen. He keeps coming back for more even after having a knee replacement surgery at the age of seventy-one.

By Don Slocum, Tony's friend

There are many old adages and wags about men being perennially children. Lore proves this to be so and it is because of the senior male propensity for attempting to recapture youth that I met Tony Naturale. While I am aware of his many exploits during his career and lifetime, it is only in the last decade that we shared together the pleasures of being young again. Tony's accomplishments on the softball and baseball diamonds are well known by his cohorts, whether in Classic 1880's games or at the Senior Olympics. While I won't and perhaps can't catalog them all, it is the following two anecdotes that stand out and speak to his character, talent, determination and commitment, demonstrated by Tony in all he does.

To be able to play senior athletics, especially competitive team sports, someone has to organize, lead and manage the players and teams. From his first encounter with me, Tony was a quiet force as a team player/manager and a league contributor. Without his continual participation to this day in these roles, the league could easily have floundered, and not tens, but conceivably hundreds of senior softball players would not have experienced the thrill of reliving the games of their childhoods.

More pertinent, and on an individual performance basis, Tony, despite sometimes physical adversity, performed at the highest competitive level. At the 2001 National Senior Games,

Tony led his team in batting average and greatly contributed to their success. Quiet, unassuming, gentle and always warm, sensitive and outgoing, Tony has been an inspiration to many and a friend to all.

ACKNOWLEDGEMENTS

I WOULD LIKE to acknowledge my wonderful children, Steven, LeeAnn and Carolyn, as well as my nephew Richard Tobin, who lived with us for a while and was more like a son to me; my sons-in-law, Kevin and Patrick; my daughter-in-law, Keiko; and all my grandchildren: Katie, Ryan, Emily, Eve, Davie and Evan; Rich's wife, Diane, and their children: Vreeland, Nolan and the precious little boy Wyatt, due in January 2004; and Richard's son, Michael, and his mom, Carmelyn. They are all my family and have put up with me during this long endeavor.

Of course, there's my brother, Victor Junior, his wife, Judy and their four sons: Tommy, Robbie, Johnny and David—all Naturales. And my sister Madie's daughter, Susan Schultz, and her husband, Glen and their two sons: Gregory and Douglas.

And a special thanks goes to my daughter LeeAnn who, even though she was so busy, took time out to help me get all the photos put through the computer and assembled for the book.

And then there are "the Citizens of Montclair, New Jersey"—most of whom made my job as a police officer more than rewarding.

My biggest joy came from actually helping people,

especially those who were on the line of being good or bad. I feel overall the rewards of assisting and guiding people overcomes the dangers and boredom of a very complex job.

And to all the policemen in every department, all over the world, who every day put their lives on the line, so that we may all have a safer environment in which to live.

Most of all, "Thank you, God, for allowing me to stay alive long enough to accomplish what I have done. I would do it all over again, just exactly as it happened."

Anthony Naturale

INTRODUCTION

This is a story about the events that occurred during my life. I am not a movie star nor a famous person, but just an average guy who had more than average things happen to me. Not only were they not average, some were downright unbelievable. I was a police officer for thirty-four years and I know most police officers could write their own book about the events that occurred during their respective careers, but this is a lot more than that.

It started out from my early childhood. It seemed that anything that could happen did happen, kind of like "Murphy's Law." But I guess we'll call this "Anthony's Law." (Hey, I'm Italian, not Irish.)

IT ALL STARTED because I used to tell humorous stories to my friends about events that happened to me when I was kid, then in the Navy and still later in the Police Department. In fact, I was only going to compile stories of the strange events that happened to and around me, and give the documentation to my children and grandchildren. But, after making an excerpt of some of the events, and showing some people, they all, unanimously, expressed to me how I should follow through and write a book. So here I am, seventy-two years of age, compiling the events of my life into a true story, in an attempt to make it readable and interesting enough for you to follow me on my journey.

While I was the "First Internal Affairs Officer" for the Montclair Police Department, I used my very good civilian friend, Frank Zaremba, to assist me. Not only was he a very trusted and honest friend, but also an excellent engineer and very qualified to help me setting up concealed cameras whenever needed. Frank has since passed away but while we worked together, he would constantly say, "Tony, I don't believe it." After a few months of working with me he said, "Tony, I believe it."

Frank named this book, so here it is, the story of my life:

"YOU'LL NEVER BELIEVE IT"

PROLOGUE

LET ME REPEAT myself as often as I can. Protection of the citizens of Montclair, New Jersey is just as important as crime in Los Angeles, Detroit or Miami: the magnitude of crime has no mirror, it continues as an open window to the world. That's why I am telling you my police experiences. The language is how we spoke in those days. When it sounds off-English, just bear with me. This is as real as it gets.

After my retirement I have had the opportunity to spend many moments with many of my fellow peers from nearby communities, as well as Montclair, to commiserate about our respective careers in law enforcement. After the first cup of coffee we, collectively speaking, agree each day on the force brought unbelievable events to each tour of duty. Just thinking about the stories told to me by one of New Jersey's finest "men in blue" convinced me any of us could have your ear for the duration of a book.

There are so many stories to be told from my early days until today. The stories I'm about to tell are all true. Some are very humorous and some are unbelievable. I have only used first names in an attempt to protect families of some of the persons who were directly involved. But before I go any further, I would also like to state that the majority of policemen are honest. It's a very difficult job and not what it appears to be to some outsiders. And no—not all policemen eat doughnuts and drink coffee all day. In fact it's a very small percentage of police officers who stray from the beaten path. I sometimes wonder why it's not a higher rate, considering all the factors involved in this very difficult and dangerous job.

I would also like to emphasize that some of the incidents aren't exactly as they occurred. I'm relating the incidents to the best of my recollection and I'm trying to keep everyone from getting too bored, so some of the stories are just similar to the actual events. The majority of police work can be very boring at times, but it goes from one extreme to the other and that's what makes it such a dangerous job, especially health-wise.

I would like to emphasize I'm not trying to degrade the Montclair Police Department. It was and still is a very good Police Department. Many of the incidents I've referred to happened many years ago and things have changed considerably, and many of the persons who may have been involved are no longer alive.

That top-notch cardiologist with a .357 Magnum sitting on the front seat of his Cadillac, following his wife through the town into the wee hours of the morning, just waiting to unload the gun into her, scheduled to perform a triple bypass at 7 A.M. still has me shaking my head; or the female pilot picked up one night for DWI, expected to sit as a captain of a major airline in the left seat of an eight-million-dollar DC-8, flying the paying public to the Coast, brings a shudder; and the most decorated United States Marine, who was brought in for beating his children. That guy or almost any officer I served with for the past thirty-four years could write a book, but this is my book and my story, believe it or not.

CHAPTER 1

IN THE BEGINNING

LIKE MANY ITALIAN-AMERICANS, I started out in Newark, New Jersey.

I was born in Saint Mary's Hospital in Orange, New Jersey in December 1931. Right after my birth, I had multiple convulsions and, according to my mother, almost didn't survive. After that rough beginning, I should have realized that my trip through life wouldn't be a very normal one, but maybe God felt I was worth saving and allowed me to continue my journey.

The following paragraph is just a rough overview and I will fill in the gaps as we go along.

We lived in Newark, New Jersey on Norfolk Street in a tenement house owned by my father's family which was lost during the Depression. We moved to Montclair, New Jersey to a three-room apartment behind a dry cleaner's shop. My mother and father worked at the cleaners, as my father was a tailor.

After about two years we moved from there to Upper Montclair. I remember we bought an old beat-up house on

Grove Street for $3,500.00. It was a two-family house, so a little money came in and we slowly renovated it.

My sister Marie and my brother Victor Junior and I all went to Watchung School, Mt. Hebron, and then Montclair High School. I graduated from Montclair High School in 1950 and worked for one year, then joined the United States Navy during the "Korean Conflict."

After being out for about six months, I joined the Montclair Police Department. I spent thirty-four years in the Police Department, going through the ranks of Patrolman, Detective, Sergeant, and Detective Lieutenant. My assignments included the Uniform Division, the Detective Bureau, Identification Bureau, Juvenile Bureau, Commander of the Detective Bureau, Court Liaison Officer, Gambling Control Officer, Internal Affairs Officer and Watch Commander.

Three days after retirement I became the Director of Safety & Security at a local hospital.

After four-and-a-half years I retired from the hospital. A few months after leaving the hospital, I started doing handyman jobs, mostly small electrical jobs. I became so busy I had to get my good friend, Bob McKeown, as my partner. We eventually had to stop taking the handymen jobs because we were getting too busy. It was getting in the way of my softball games, so we just did the electrical jobs. Eventually Bob moved and we moved, so that ended our small business together. Now all I did was play baseball, softball and bowl, and once in a while, do a small electrical job.

At this writing I am seventy-two years of age and still going strong. Fortunately I'm in pretty good health and, oh yes, I am somewhat fanatical about exercise. I do fifty push-ups, 400 sit-ups and do the "karate" leg exercises daily. Actually I was going to write a book a few years ago on physical fitness but that never worked out. I may still attempt it; but now it will have to be "Fitness for Seniors."

My biggest love (just ask my wife) is softball. From March

to November I play four games a week; played in the "Senior Olympics" four times, once in the sixty-year-old group, and twice in the sixty-fives. Next year, God willing, I hope to play in the seventies at the Senior Olympics in Norfolk, Virginia.

I also started hardball this year, playing once a week. I hope to play in the "Roy Hobbs Seniors World Series" which takes place in Florida every year, and hope to play in Cooperstown in September 2003.

I also bowl twice a week, once with the Knights of Columbus and once with the girls from the hospital (nurses). But I don't want to get too far ahead, so let me tell you how it all began.

At the turn of the century, as the Southern Italian migration to the United States began, a small majority settled in Newark, New Jersey's largest city, some eight miles west of Manhattan. Thus Newark became one of the first cities in the country outside of New York with a huge Italian immigrant community.

Early on the migration was slow, but soon began to gain momentum. In 1880, Italians residing in the city numbered 407. In the next three decades, between 1880 and 1910, approximately 20,000 newcomers were added. A large Italian quarter grew up in the East Ward, which is sometimes called the "Ironbound District," and that included Norfolk Street, where we all lived in a large tenement house (owned by my father's family) which was sadly lost during the Depression.

Vito Naturale (my father) was born on January 22, 1905 in Bella, Italy, a small village just north of Naples, the second of three sons and a daughter of Vito and Maria Parisi Naturale. He came to the United States at the age of seven, landing on Ellis Island with his mother, brother Angelo, and his cousin Carmine. They stayed with relatives until their father and other relatives arrived. They eventually ended up in the Ironbound section of Newark, New Jersey. None of the boys finished school because times were very tough and they all had to chip in and work. They pooled their money and eventually they were able to buy a tenement house on Norfolk Street in Newark, New Jersey.

Josephine Lemongelli, my mother (that's right, Lemongelli), was born on June 8, 1912 in Camden, New Jersey. She was one of thirteen children of Caroline Fortunato Lemongelli and Vito Lemongelli, who also migrated from Italy.

My mother's father, Vito, was Grandma Carolyn's second husband. She had been married to Vito's cousin, Anthony Farano, but he had died at an early age. Carolyn had eleven of her thirteen children (including my mom) with Vito, and the first two with his cousin. Sound confusing? Wait until you read the whole book . . . you will really be confused and probably won't believe it.

Grandpa Vito almost didn't make it either. As a very young man, he fell from the top of a three-story building while working as a construction worker, crushing many bones in his face and other parts of his body. He, in fact, was the first person they ever did "skin grafting" on, and the doctors who performed the operations wrote a book on it. The book is kept in the hospital files as a reference tool. Grandpa Lemongelli lived to the ripe old age of ninety-nine.

I don't know how my mother and father met, but they obviously did and were married. She was sixteen and he was twenty-three. He worked in a small tailor shop in Newark just off the line of East Orange. She used to walk from her house on Amherst Street in East Orange to the store after school. I don't know how long they went out, but they were married on November 4, 1928.

I was born on December 19, 1931, in Orange, New Jersey; I have one brother, Victor Junior, and a sister, Marie (Madie). Neither my brother nor I could say Marie, and Madie is what came out. It stuck with her for her entire lifetime. This seemed to be a pretty normal existence; however, when I have completed this story there may be some doubt about it.

As I had stated, it all started out in Newark, New Jersey.

We all lived in the large tenement house on Norfolk Street. What I remember seemed to be pretty good. It was during the Depression and all our cousins lived in the apartments around us. There were about fifteen cousins and it was a fun time because we were very young and all we did was play together.

We didn't have much money but we didn't need much; no cars, telephones or TVs. We would have spaghetti every Sunday and Thursday and all eat together in one apartment. I swear I thought that spaghetti commercial was my mother calling me. She would yell "Anthony" louder than that lady in the commercial. (Today I never eat spaghetti and my Irish wife wonders why.)

Of course this lifestyle wouldn't last too long. It was during the Depression and the family was losing the building because no one had much money and couldn't pay much rent, so slowly we all started moving to different places. I must say I really miss those days. I believe I was about five or six years old when we moved.

CHAPTER 2

MONTCLAIR, NEW JERSEY

WE MOVED FROM Newark, New Jersey to Montclair and rented a small store at 25 Valley Road, which my parents used as a dry cleaners. It had a three-room apartment in the rear.

Now, when they rented the place the landlord said we could have the place if there were only two children, and of course my mother says, "Oh, that's perfect, we only have two children." Naturally, you know who was left behind . . . right, me. Here I was, only around six years old, and I get farmed out. I should have realized, even at that young age that my life was going to be, shall we say, "different." As my son Steven says today . . ."unique."

I was left behind at my grandmother's house at night, but I did stay in Montclair during the day. I guess you could say I was in "night care." This situation went on for about a year until one day the landlord, Mrs. Kaveny (who used to see me there all the time), started questioning us. She very easily figured it out when my brother Victor said,

"He's my brother, not my cousin." In the beginning my mother had told her sometimes her 'nephew' would stay with us . . . which was me. The very nice landlord yelled at my mother and stated, "How could you leave your cute little boy behind like that?" (I thought the same thing.) All of a sudden I liked Mrs. Kaveny.

My brother Victor just reminded me of another story about that same landlord, who would always come out with a banana for all of us but my brother would always say, "I have to check with Mama to see if it's rotten." This happened many times and the landlord would just smile.

Anyway, I returned to my family and was taken out of "night care," and I became Mrs. Kaveny's favorite. (I didn't care if the banana was rotten or not).

It's amazing how I can remember some of those events and today can't remember where my reading glasses or my keys are.

It was a nice area in those days, right off of Bloomfield Avenue and behind the old Montclair Theater, which is now the municipal parking lot. Across the street were the Fire and Police Departments, and you would constantly see the police cars and fire engines leaving with their sirens and lights going. I sometimes wonder, as I used to imagine myself going on the calls with them, if that was when it was instilled in my very young and susceptible brain to become a policeman or fireman. I do know when I was a fireman in the Navy, for a short time, I couldn't stand intense smoke so that eliminated the Fire Department. Who knows?

After staying there for a couple of years, we moved to Upper Montclair . . . some jump from the three-room apartment. It was a two-family house but each floor had three bedrooms. My brother and I still had the same bedroom, while my sister got her own. It sure was an improvement from the three of us sleeping on a pull-out couch. Eventually the tenants moved out and we had the whole house. This was like a mansion compared to what we had.

Now this is when Upper Montclair was Upper-Upper Montclair. We moved to 427 Grove Street, just off of Wildwood Avenue, and the only place Italians lived in Upper Montclair was on Wildwood Avenue. In fact, they called the lower end of Wildwood Avenue "Little Italy." We lived just around the corner from Wildwood, so because we were Italian, we could have been considered a part of Little Italy.

I went to Watchung School and then to Mt. Hebron (which had only about twenty Italians, and of that total was my brother, sister and me). We had quite a few skirmishes with the "Medigans" (that's what we called the non-Italians). When we got to high school it changed quite a bit, but a lot of the factions still stuck together. Actually, most of my immediate friends were non-Italians (medigans). However, living on Grove Street, just around the corner from Wildwood Avenue, some of the Italians didn't consider us qualified for living in "Little Italy." I guess you could say we were Medi-Italians.

Even though my mother worked all day, it was my sister Marie (Madie), although only two years older than me, who was the boss. She acted like an Army Sergeant over my brother and me, and we had a pretty good life. When I look back at it now, I realize she didn't do such a bad job. We couldn't touch her because if either of us did, my mom and dad would hear about it as soon they got home. In those days it wasn't illegal to use a belt or the point of a high-heeled shoe (my mother's favorite) to beat some sense into us. At the end of the day, when my parents came home, Madie had a list of bad things she would report. They wouldn't even listen . . . they would just whack us. My brother (Junior) always got the worst of it because he was a step slower than I. I had to do something. This just wasn't fair.

One day I got a bright idea and asked my friend Bob

Tully to "beat on" my sister a little. After all, my parents couldn't "beat on" him. Well, this worked out pretty good until the old guy across the street, Mr. Covello, saw Bob beating up Madie; he came running across the street and started whacking Junior and me with his cane, for allowing my friend to do this. It was the last time we did that. The old guy could really swing his cane, and on top of that we still got the shoe when my mother got home.

In fact, my sister got along so well with Mr. Covello that he had his son-in-law Lou Monte, the singer, come with his guitar and sing "Happy Birthday" at her sixteenth birthday party; she was thrilled. He was just becoming famous for his rendition of "I'll Be Down To Get You In A Taxi, Honey."

Another incident really sticks in my mind with Madie: Vic and I were fighting in the small bathroom adjacent to the hallway and she was getting ready for a date with Charlie Fergus, who was sitting in the living room, waiting for her. She wasn't aware he was there for their date, and came running from her bedroom into the bathroom ranting and raving at us. First she flung me out of the room, and then literally threw Vic out. Charlie could see the whole thing. He saw us both come flying out and then she, in her curlers, right after us. Well, Charlie got quite an earful and we all thought he would never return; but he did come back. In fact, they were married not long after. I guess Charlie liked the dominant-type woman.

Sadly, Madie contracted fatal cancer just a few years ago and died approximately one year later. During the last year of Madie's life, my wife, Madeline, cared for her day and night when she came to live with us . . . spending meaningful and tender moments. My sister really went out very courageously. I'm so glad we had that time together. This time Madeline was the Sergeant but a very gentle one.

Madeline, with her indomitable spirit, loving ways and ever-warm smile, has the unique gift of truly knowing how to take care of people above and beyond the call of duty.

Sadly, her mother had died when she was only ten years old and she automatically acted like a "Little Mother" to her five brothers. As the years passed she took care of her brother, Bill Tobin, and later on Richard Tobin, so she certainly had the experience.

My very first day at Watching School was quite eventful when this kid, Arthur Muhler, came up to me and said, "Are you the new kid?" As I began to answer, he punched me straight in the nose, causing it to bleed. I thought I had left Newark (we used to fight there all the time). Here I was in Upper Montclair, on the first day, and had to fight. Well, believe it or not, Art became one of my best friends and to this day, we are still good friends.

The next day, another kid, Bob Tully, came up to me and started wrestling with me. We actually rolled right onto Watchung Avenue. I remember this very vividly because traffic stopped both ways and motorists were becoming quite angry because they couldn't move as we kept rolling back and forth across the road. It finally ended in a draw, to the delight of the delayed motorists. I thought I even heard some of them applaud. Bob also became one of my best friends. (I guess you had to fight each other to become good friends). Bob and I also were very competitive in all sports throughout school; he was a great athlete.

We both even tried being altar boys at Saint Cassian's Church. Unfortunately for us, but fortunately for the Saint Cassian's parishioners, it didn't work out. One day Bob Tully, Jimmie Nasisi and I went to see Father Brown and Father Launders and convinced them that we were cut out to be altar boys. We lasted about two weeks. It ended while we, as altar boys, were serving Mass on an Easter Sunday; when Jimmie and I looked at each other and started laughing and couldn't stop. Bob saw us and also started in. Father Brown very calmly ushered the three of us from the altar, out of the church and explained to us that we were not cut out to be altar boys. Our parents were mortified and yes, I still am a Catholic.

Sadly, I no longer have my childhood friend Bob Tully as, at the very young age of forty, he died of cancer, leaving four children and a spouse. I would drive his wife, Carmella, to Sloan Kettering Hospital in New York City a couple of times a week. I was working nights at the time and was able to do it. Each time I saw my childhood buddy he had a smile, and was always upbeat. I was talking to him and holding his hand when, without warning, he just closed his eyes and died. It's a moment I won't forget.

Because Bob was in the hospital for so long, many bills mounted for the family. I decided to get some people together and hold a benefit for the family to ease their burden. I contacted some of the football players from the 1949 Montclair High School State Championship team, of which Bob Tully was a starting end, to arrange a fund-raising benefit. The response was overwhelming; there was a great turnout, not only from the team, but many of his fellow high school friends. We were able to make quite a dent in the bills that had accumulated.

Jack Sar, the other starting end for the team, gave a very touching speech at the end of the benefit.

> "Bob will always be with us; even now I understand, and I am sure you do too . . . or you would not have come today . . . that we had a championship football team because we stuck together when a fellow 'footballer' was in need. Hence, we are here today to, once again, remember we are still that same team because Bob Tully was, and still is, a real champion and lives on in our hearts forever."

Another friend we still see today is Ken Grieco. The first

day I met him he kicked me in the shins. Quite a soccer player, he constantly mistook my shins for the ball (so he says). He had the pointiest shoes. I think he must have sharpened them somehow. Ken recently reminded me that he used to kick everyone in the shins. In fact, he kicked Charlie Johnson so hard Charlie had to be taken to the emergency room and required numerous stitches to close the wound. Charlie's mother actually came into Ken's classroom and admonished him in front of the entire class. Kenny said he never kicked Charlie again. Charlie Johnson went on to become a very successful businessman as the owner of Franklin Funds. Just recently I saw his picture on the front page of *Barron's* business magazine.

Probably my closest friend today is Donald Stake. He was my best man at my wedding, but is probably best known for putting a stink bomb in the Bellevue Theater. We were in the eighth grade then and the whole theater had to be evacuated. Don looked like such an angel and no one suspected him of putting the stink bomb in the theater. Don said he wants to write the last chapter of this book. "No way, Don. You're too sneaky." Don and his wife, Dot, are still our good friends. They had twin daughters, Bonnie and Sharon, and a son, Drew. I am godfather to one of the twins. I still don't know which one, as they looked so much alike. While at the Jersey Shore just recently, Sharon Silva, the elder twin by one minute, now at the young age of fifty-two, remarked, "I'm sure Uncle Tony was holding me because I'm just like him and Aunt Dorothy held Bonnie because she's the quiet one like her." I can't argue with that. She has to be right.

Another close friend is Tommy DelloRusso. We met in high school, and played alongside each other in the line on the football team. I often said Tommy hit harder than anyone else on our team. I was shifted to fullback my senior year and had to run against him in practice a few times. Boy, did that hurt. Tom (five feet five inches) was so low to the ground you couldn't see him until he hit you. One thing I vividly remember about Tommy was when a Marine Recruiter came to the high school trying to recruit from the school, and asked if anyone had any questions and Tommy raised up his hand.

"Would you please stand up?" The instructor asked.

I yelled out, "He *is* standing up."

This got a big laugh because he actually was standing up. Tom was just about as wide as he was tall. He really was interested in the Marines because right after graduation he joined up. He then went on to Korea and made quite a name for himself, earning many medals after being wounded at the Choson Reservoir. I guess size doesn't really matter. Tommy was really tough and has a big heart. Tommy and his wife, Olga, are our good friends and we still see them from time to time.

Donald, Art and I tried to join the unit Tom was in but fortunately for us, they were leaving for Camp Pendleton in a few weeks; there wasn't enough time to train new recruits. This probably saved our lives, because many of the Marines in Tom's unit were killed in Korea during battle. We may not have been as lucky as Tommy.

I have to include as one of my old friends Jay McMillan, who lived on Wildwood Avenue (the upper part—not Little Italy; he's not Italian). We used to walk to school together from Watchung to Mt. Hebron and to the high school. The incident I remember most about Jay was when I was an usher at the Bellevue Theater. We had it planned that I would leave the exit door ajar so they could sneak in. I was able to do it but one of the other ushers saw that it was ajar and pulled it shut. In the meantime, the guys came up the fire escape. I believe it was Art, Bob, Jimmy and Jay. They were banging on the door and the walking policeman spotted them and chased them . . . eventually catching Jay. He actually fired a shot at them. Poor Jay became very frightened and stopped. Hence, the policeman nabbed "Jay the Perp" and caught him. At police headquarters he gave up the other guys and told them the door was supposed to be left open by me. I was fired from my job and we were all put on probation. Jay still calls me and many other of his old classmates on their respective birthdays. I don't know how he remembers the dates after all these years . . . but he does.

I mention all these friends because, over the years, we still continue to connect. I think it is somewhat rare for friends to stay together that long. There are many others but these are some of the most memorable.

I should have known my life would be a little different. My mother was more like "Gracie Allen" than Gracie herself. She was always at the wrong place at the wrong time and so was I (like mother, like son).

I can still vividly remember this one incident with Mama, because I see the scar every day. We didn't go out and buy a turkey for Thanksgiving; we bought it well before, fed it and then ate it. Yep, we were different, all right. None of us wanted to eat the turkey after having had it for a pet; not only that, I had to help my mother kill the turkey. She had me hold it around the neck while she cut the head off. (Where are the animal rights people when you need them?) The only problem was in this one case she wasn't very accurate, almost chopping my middle finger off. Mom ran off screaming, the turkey ran off headless while I was holding my hand tightly to stop the bleeding. Believe it or not, everything turned out fine. I had about three stitches, we all had our turkey dinner (a little later than usual), and everyone laughed about it.

Whenever I look at my right finger, I see the scar and recall the incident. Everyone else in the family has heard the story numerous times. I try not to look at the scar before I eat turkey. It tastes much better that way.

Carolina and
Vito Lemongelli

Fifty years later . . .

Victor and
Josephine
Naturale
(Mom and Pop)

Jack and
Lee Tobin
(Madeline's
Mom and Dad)

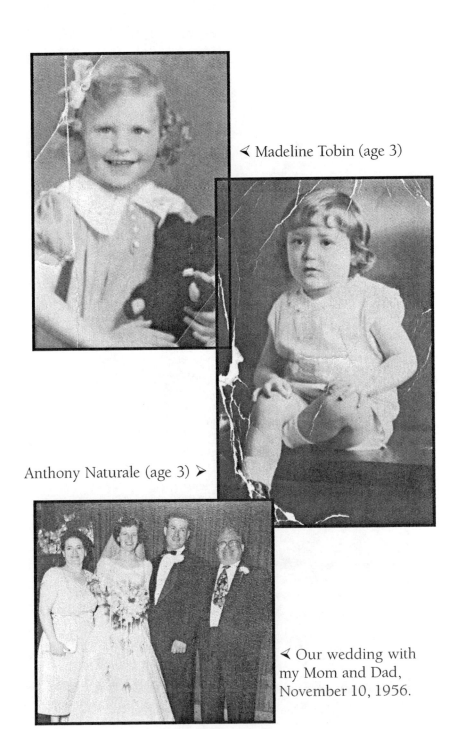

◄ Madeline Tobin (age 3)

Anthony Naturale (age 3) ➤

◄ Our wedding with
my Mom and Dad,
November 10, 1956.

Madeline
Tobin,
age 8

Madeline and her
dad Jack Tobin at
Lake Erskive 1954.
And she's still cute!

Eighth grade class at Mount Hebron School. From the bottom, 4th one in the 4th row on the left is me!

◄ Me, age 14

1949 State Football Champions—Montclair High School

Clifton
Bloomfield

Coaches:
Butch Fortunato
and
Clary Anderson

Football players at our 50th reunion at Upper Montclair Country Club.

USS Siboney CVE112

Discharged
from USN June
1, 1955 ➤

Smitty and I
having our last
cup of coffee, in
Norfolk, VA . . .
just before our
discharge. ▲

◄ Rookie Year 1957

L to R—Richard Tait, Ronald Lappe, George Gilruth and me graduating from Police Academy—Cedar Grove, NJ, May 1956. ⋀

CHAPTER 3

FIRST POLICE ENCOUNTER

MY FIRST ENCOUNTER with "the police" was when I was in the eighth grade. Our dog, King, was run over in front of our house by a speeding car on Grove Street. When the police car arrived, the officer actually took his jacket off, put it over the dog and started consoling me. This act of compassion really impressed me and I never forgot it. Up to this point the police were "The Enemy."

I started talking to this policeman and believe it or not, this same policeman (Gus Roesch) was the one who delivered the letter to my home when I was appointed to the police department. I later became his partner in the radio car for a short time.

Another incident that sticks out in my mind was the "Ice Cream Caper." This occurred while we were going to Mt. Hebron School (eighth grade). I don't know what possessed us but we felt like ice cream that night and none of us had any money. We borrowed Tommy's car because we didn't have one. We decided to go into the basement of Mt. Hebron School and help ourselves to some ice cream. We parked his car right in front of the school. (Some plan, huh?) We walked right into the cafeteria area because one of the screens was off of the window and would you believe it—the window was unlocked. It was an open invitation we could not resist.

About six of us went in and opened up the freezer and started eating the ice cream. I don't know whose idea it was (it wasn't mine), but we decided to take the big ten-gallon cans; I think there were three of them. We actually ate one whole ten-gallon can of the ice cream and now had two cans left and didn't know what to do with them. One of the guys, Jim, said he had a big freezer and could empty one of the cans in it. That left us with one. No one wanted it so I said I would get rid of it somehow.

The next day the school came out with a notice: "No ice cream for lunch." In fact, they called the police and reported that it was stolen. Wow, who would do anything like that? In fact, one of our crew even offered the suggestion that maybe it had melted. I don't mind telling you we were all pretty scared.

Now, you probably want to know what I did with my ten-gallon can. Well, in effect it had melted . . . right into all the mouths of the neighborhood dogs. I put it in an old junk car my dad had on the side of the garage. I very cleverly (ha-ha) left the windows open, figuring all the animals in the area would get a treat. And they did.

Our "caper" would have been over with if our friend Jim hadn't tried to put all that ice cream into the small ice-cube trays in his refrigerator. "Now come on, Jim, what's-a matter with you?" Well, his mother saw all this vanilla fudge ice cream dripping out of her trays and onto the kitchen floor. Would you believe it—she had just finished reading the *Montclair Times*. And the front page read, "Thieves steal 30 gallons of vanilla fudge ice cream from Mt. Hebron School." She immediately questioned her son and it took all of about two minutes before he gave everyone up. I guess it must be right—"There is no honor among thieves."

We all received probation and were fined enough to pay

for the ice cream. Fortunately for us, we were juveniles and it didn't actually give us a record. It was a well-learned lesson. Actually I never really did like vanilla fudge. Now I hate it.

Another story I probably shouldn't tell—but what the hell, we've passed the "statute of limitations," so I'll tell it. Bob, Art, Jimmy, and I believe Tommy, all went into the Gulf station on Valley Road in Upper Montclair on Halloween. We all used to hang out at this station and knew Bill, the owner, quite well. We figured we would play a prank on him: we snuck up on him, put a burlap bag over his head and tied him up (some prank). We all had masks on, so he couldn't recognize us. We took all the candy he had in the office for the kids (mean, huh?) and then we left him.

A few minutes later, we called the police, stating there had been a hold-up and a man was tied up. We watched from a distance as the police arrived and untied him. Boy, he was a physical wreck. The police couldn't figure out why no money was taken and the case remained unsolved. We did give all the candy to some young kids who were walking by (kind of like Robin Hood).

I don't know why I even included this story because as I look at it now, it doesn't seem funny. Some of you are even wondering how I became a policeman, let alone the Internal Affairs Officer. I wonder myself sometimes, but remember this . . . to be a good policeman you have to think like a criminal. How else would we have such a good record for catching the thieves?

That gas station reminded me of another incident that revolved around it. I was going pretty steady with a girl named Joan. I met Joan when she worked as a waitress at the "Candy Cane" at Watchung Plaza. She was really a very pretty girl and all the guys who hung out at the Plaza were dying to get to Joan. I was very fortunate she picked me. Maybe it had something to do with me not drinking because all the guys would meet there and then go out for a few drinks. I would just sit there and drink Cokes all night and when it was closing time, I would ask her if she wanted a ride home because, as she lived downtown, I knew she had to catch a bus. Considering the late hour, I feared for her safety.

I guess I was kind of a "schemer" at that young age. Heck, I didn't even have a license—I was only sixteen. I always had a car but my parents didn't know it. We would push it out of our driveway so my parents wouldn't hear it and once we got to the street, we would start it up. When I brought it back later at night I would turn the engine off and coast it in the driveway so they couldn't hear me. I remember my mother always saying, "This car is very bad on gas. I'm always filling it up and the next day it's on empty." I would say, "Yeah, Mom, these old cars are very bad on gas. Maybe we should get a newer car—a little quieter one." Sorry, Mom.

I was a junior, and Joan was a senior (I was mature for my age) when I started going out with her. Sometimes the guys would all meet at the station and then go out. A few times I would have Joan with me and she really didn't like going out with my friends as she was the only girl, so I would ask her if she wanted to wait there and she would. Sometimes we would be gone for a couple of hours and Joan would just stay in the station and talk to Bill and his helper, Jim, and I would usually bring a pizza back for all of us.

After about the third time I did this, Jim came up to me and asked me if I was serious about Joan. I told him I really wasn't. That night when I took her home, she said Jim had asked her out. I said, "Do you want to go out with him?"

She said, "If you don't mind."

So she went out with him. About a month later she told me she really liked Jim and he had asked her to marry him. Wow, I was relieved. I'm so glad it was to him. She was a very nice girl but just too old for me. I always knew she wanted to get married because she would talk about it so much. I would always change the subject because it was not even part of my equation.

A year later they did get married and never even invited

me to the wedding. Imagine that?

About ten years later, as a detective with the Montclair Police Department, I was assigned, while on a coordinated drug raid, to the East Orange Police Department, and I ran into Joan's husband. Jim was now a sergeant with the East Orange Police. We talked for a short time and he told me the good news: Joan and he were expecting their fifth child. Wow, was she fertile or what?

Back to where we were:

I still wanted to be a policeman more than anything, and probably the most influential person was "Smitty," an elderly policeman who walked the Avenue beat right by my parents' family business, Ace Cleaners at 301 Bloomfield Avenue. He would talk to me all the time and tell me stories about the job. It was he who actually convinced me to take the job.

The irony of this is a few years later when I came on the Police Department, Smitty had retired a few months earlier—I was actually his replacement. He was so happy to see me get the job. He was a good friend and a big influence on me. Thanks, Smitty.

Most of my junior high and high school days were devoted to football, baseball, basketball, and even soccer. I must admit, I was pretty good in baseball; maybe that's why, at age seventy-two, I'm still playing both hardball and softball. It was probably my best sport and I believe I still have the record for hitting the longest ball from Mt. Hebron School playground over the fence, across the street and onto the roof of the school. Last time I checked, the ball is still on the roof. I don't know what I ate that day but I remember I had four hits, including two home runs and two doubles. When I did this, they immediately put me on the ninth grade team (I was in eighth grade at the time).

Now every time I drive by there, whoever is in the car with me at the time gets the whole story. Actually it amazes me now, when I mentally measure the distance, because it has to be well over 300 feet. Usually every time I go by there,

I add about fifty feet to the distance it traveled. I wish I could hit it that far today. I'll go more into my softball and baseball stories later on.

CHAPTER 4

MONTCLAIR HIGH SCHOOL

HIGH SCHOOL SEEMED easy because I didn't do much. In fact, the entire three years (10-12 grades), I don't believe I took a book home (not proud of that). My history teacher said she used to teach in the penal system and that dealing with prisoners was easier than dealing with me. I never took it very seriously as I loved to kid around . . . I guess it was always at the wrong time. She would certainly be surprised that I actually graduated from Montclair State College (which is now a university) with a 3.0 average and actually ended up with a teaching certificate and am qualified to teach history from grades six to twelve (which was that teacher's subject!). I don't think she would ever believe this fact. Actually I was forty-five years old when I graduated, so maybe she might believe it. (I was forty when I started.)

A few years ago, that same teacher saw me directing traffic in front of Montclair High School. She gave me a scrutinizing hard look and said, "Anthony Naturale, is that really you?"

Well, at least I got that question right. I said, "Yes, it's me."

She said, "You have some nerve becoming a policeman."

What could I say? I just crossed her and kept my mouth shut—that was more than I did in her class. My wife, Madeline, who was also crossing the street at the same time, was a witness to this infamous remark.

At this point in time all I really cared about was sports. In football, I was the only tenth-grade lineman to get a blue shirt (varsity). I really had one very good day in practice, making about six tackles in a row. I remember Coach Clary Anderson saying, "Can't anybody stop that little guy!" After that remark from Clary, the two linemen in front of me, Willie Love and Cokey DeNicola, both blocked me and both landed on top of me. I have a scar on my left wrist from that encounter. It seemed, when my teammates landed on me, I chipped a bone in my left wrist. Many years later, when a doctor operated on me, he stated this was the result of a very heavy weight landing on my wrist. I'll say it was heavy. They were each well over 225 pounds. I wasn't that small, but compared to the first-string linemen I was.

My varsity stint was very short-lived, because a few days later, the "bone doctor" stated he detected a heart murmur during my physical. What does a bone doctor know about the heart anyway? Of course my own doctor said I was fine, and there were no signs of a murmur. But try telling that to my mother, who had been against me playing football from the start. It took me the whole year to convince my mother to let me play in my junior year, but by then Clary (the coach) and I were not on the best of terms.

I think everyone knew Clary Anderson. He was quite a coach, with a great record, and even had the town arena named after him when he died. I guess I picked the wrong coach to argue with.

For a while, I felt like a yo-yo because Butch Fortunato, the line coach, would put me in and then Clary would take me out. I got along great with Butch. Butch was quite a player in his day at Fordham, playing with Vince Lombardi and the infamous "Seven Blocks of Granite." He wrote in my yearbook, *Best wishes, Nat, I always admired your courage and it was a pleasure working with a boy that enjoyed contact the way you did. I wanted to say,.* "Hey Butch, I didn't actually enjoy it—it actually hurt," but by then the season was over.

Because of that problem with Clary in football, it affected me in baseball. (He was also the baseball coach.) I also made the varsity in the tenth grade and was playing behind a senior first baseman, Bob Richardson. Now that means when he leaves, the guy behind him should, at the very least, get the shot, right? Well, it never happened. He played a guy ahead of me, right from the start.

Well, there went my baseball career. I could see the writing on the wall. I didn't want to waste my time sitting on the bench, so I quit and took up boxing. I even got my amateur license and went into the Diamond Gloves.

My first fight in the Diamond Gloves was also very humorous. I think my whole class came to Paterson to see me fight. Now I wasn't skinny, but when the guy fighting me came in the ring, I thought I was in the ring with a gorilla. He was so hairy and old. He was in the Army on leave and had a family in the first row. Now what was a seventeen-year-old kid doing fighting this guy? I was and I seemed to be doing pretty good until I dropped my mouthpiece. Did you ever try and pick anything up with sixteen-ounce boxing gloves on? I tried and every time I bent down to pick it up, he would punch me as I bent down. Now where was the ref? He should have held the fight up until I got my mouthpiece in, but he didn't. Anyway, I guess it seemed funny to everybody watching who were howling, but it wasn't funny to me. I got so tired bending up and down trying to pick up my mouthpiece I lost the fight. My manager said I hit him more but I looked more tired than him. Well, of course I was. Tired of bending up and down. That was my last fight until I went into the Navy.

I guess I was born to be a policeman and not any kind of athlete. Everything was pointing that way. My basketball career didn't last long either. (We had a different coach.) In junior high I was one of the bigger guys at five feet nine inches, but in high school, that was quite small. It didn't make much sense wasting all that time sitting on the bench, so that ended that.

One football story I think should be told. I was a junior at the time and we were playing Kearny High School. Alex Webster, who later became a great player for the New York Giants, was playing fullback and he was just ripping our line apart. It was near the end of the fourth quarter and somehow we were leading 8-6. Butch put me in the middle of the line and said, "Tony, we have to stop Webster."

"OK, Coach," I said, thinking I would stop him single-handedly.

Well, it didn't quite work out as I wanted it to. The next play he ran down the middle right over me. I had my arms wrapped around him but he just shook me off. (Hey—he was a great player.) He proceeded to run over our All-State linebacker, Joe, and then over our safety, Eugene, and continued on for a touchdown. Needless to say, they ended up winning the game with a score of 13-8. The irony is that Orange beat them and we beat Orange, so it was a three-way tie for the State Championship in 1948.

Of course, everyone knows Alex Webster went on to become a great professional football player and play for the New York Giants. We really had a great team and won the State Championship all three years, 1947-1948-1949.

Another play that sticks out in my mind was the very last play of my high school football career. It was against Bloomfield High School on Thanksgiving Day. Because of the extreme competitive rivalry between Montclair and Bloomfield, both players and fans could not wait for the season-ending game. And here I was, playing fullback, a lineman's dream, and actually carrying the ball. Of course, being a lineman all of my years (except the last three games, my senior year . . . when I played fullback), you dream of scoring a touchdown.

So here it is, the last play of the year, and I get the call to run right down the middle; I just put my head down and ran as hard as I could. To my surprise I knocked down the linebacker and ran right over him and was picking up speed as the safety (the last man I had to get by) came charging directly at me. Again I put my head down, ran straight into him, knocking him down. But, as he was falling, he grabbed my helmet. It came off and I kept running down the field. Now I had about twenty yards to go and no one was near me. I made the mistake of turning around to look at the guy I just ran over. It was very funny and I even began to laugh, because he looked so surprised and was just sitting on the ground looking, in disbelief, as he held my helmet in his hand. When I turned back towards the goal line, which was now about two yards away, my feet somehow got tangled up and I tripped. I reached out, and as I fell towards the goal line, I pushed the ball as far forward as I could reach. I landed, with a resounding thud, flat on my face; the ball was about six inches short, as the gun sounded that the game was over.

To this day, I still can't believe I didn't score. That was my very last game of football.

I wasn't very serious in high school and was always kidding around. Now I wish I had paid more attention. In fact I wasn't even voted Class Clown—I came in second. The guy who was voted Class Clown, Bob Doremus, became the first pilot to be shot down in Viet Nam and the first prisoner of war.

I guess he knew how to be serious when he had to be. He was a real hero.

Things were happening to me I couldn't believe, and there were many more to come. I did graduate; however, my grades weren't good enough to get in college at this time, so I went to work.

CHAPTER 5

UNITED STATES NAVY

AFTER WORKING FOR Bob Frei, the electrician, for about one year, I went into the Navy. I say went because I *went;* I didn't join. I went with my alleged friend "Skippy" Rizzie. He asked me to take a ride with him to New York City because he was going to "join the Navy." So I went with him for a ride . . . a four-year ride.

You probably think, how could anyone go for a ride and end up in the Navy? You'll never believe it, but here's what happened.

Skip went into the room to take the test. I stood outside in another room, reading a magazine. A very nice polite sailor came over to me and asked what I was doing there. I told him I was waiting for my buddy. He said very nicely, "Look, he's going to be in there about an hour, so why don't you go in there also instead of waiting out here by yourself? You can take the test just to sharpen your skills and then tell them you're not joining. You have thirty days to decide. This way, who knows? You may still want to join up."

I thought that sounded reasonable so I went in and took

the test. I was planning to go to Panzer College the next semester, and this would give me good practice. When we were finished, the very clever sailor came over to me and said, "You did so well, I guarantee you will go to school in the Navy, and when you get out you can go to college—free."

Then my alleged friend, "Skip," started working on me and would you believe it? I joined up. Well, I did have the thirty days to change my mind and I knew that's what I would do.

When I got home I told my parents, and they seemed quite happy thinking that maybe I finally found my way.

About three weeks later, they had a big surprise party for me (I guess they were really glad I was leaving). Many friends and relatives were there. Boy, what a great party. I got all kinds of gifts and money.

A couple of days later I gave them another surprise. I told them I wasn't going into the Navy—I was going to enter Panzer College the next semester. Now would you believe it? They were quite angry. Hey, I was going to college. They should be happy. Then they said I would have to return all the gifts and money. Now that was a problem. The gifts, no problem; but most of the money was gone. I was wining and dining all my friends (including Skippy). Two hundred-plus dollars was a lot of money at that time and there was no way I could dig it up. So I did the only thing I could do: join the Navy. Hell, I couldn't even swim. (Still can't swim today.) I was probably the only sailor in the entire Navy who couldn't swim, but I never told anybody.

I entered the Navy in June 1951, and what hurt most was that Skip didn't leave . . . well, not before me anyway. The funniest thing happened when Skip did arrive a few weeks later at the same boot camp in Great Lakes, Illinois.

We were marching in unison when his bus arrived. I saw him getting off and looked over towards him, for just an instant. Would you believe it, in that instant my marching column stopped and because I looked over towards Skip at the same instant, I kept on marching. Oh well, it's not too hard to figure out what happened next. Did you ever see dominos when one falls over? Yep—that's exactly what happened. I bumped into the guy in front of me and so on and so on. Actually it was quite funny, except the Chief in the front column wasn't laughing. The sailor at the end of the bump bumped into the Chief. Boy, was that Chief angry. Hey, it was only a slight bump. He didn't even knock him down.

Skip got me in trouble again. I don't know why I kept him as a friend. Luckily he was assigned to a different ship than me. We could have lost the war ourselves. One guy even said he thought we were spies for the enemy. Honest to God—we weren't.

The recruiter was right. After boot camp I got into electrical school, but for only three months; not much out of four years. I was assigned to Great Lakes, Illinois, for boot camp, then went to electrical school for the three months at the same camp. It's got to be the deadest spot in the world, and probably the coldest. It was colder there in September and October than it was in the winter in New Jersey.

One good thing happened while I was there—well, good for a while, anyway.

I met a really nice girl at the USO. I never thought she would go for me because she was a billionaire's daughter. We went together the whole time I was in electrical school. She was really nice and we both talked about getting married and the whole works. Well, I finished school and got sent to Norfolk, Virginia. We were writing back and forth for months and making plans for her to come down to Norfolk. All the guys on the ship would relentlessly kid me, saying no rich girl would go for a measly enlisted man. I tried to tell them they were wrong. One guy said to me, "Don't write her back and see what happens." So I said, "OK." I didn't write her for about a month, then I finally did. She never answered me.

A couple of weeks later I telephoned her. She was very

cold to me but said she would write me. And she did. About
one week later she wrote me a nice "Dear John" letter, but
this said, "Dear Tony, I'm sorry, but I'm engaged to be married.
I never heard from you and I met someone else."

Well, that was that. I guess she couldn't have cared for
me too much to get engaged in that short period of time. To
think, I almost became a billionaire's husband. Well, I'm not
sorry because I think I got a better deal marrying my wife,
Madeline Tobin, the "Ice Man's" daughter. Of course we're
not billionaires, but who needs money? We had plenty of
free ice.

While I was in Norfolk, Virginia, I was assigned to a carrier
escort, the "Siboney." This carrier was quite large and was
like a floating hotel. We would go out to sea for weeks at a
time, so we played a lot of basketball on the hanger deck and
football on the flight deck. One thing sticks in my mind:
While we were playing football on the flight deck, I threw a
long pass to this guy and led him just a little too much. What
a try he made—better than some pros. The only problem
was he ran out of flight deck. I don't know why any of us
laughed because he could have been killed, but believe it or
not, he never hit the water. He hit an overhanging deck about
twenty feet below. (I find myself laughing as I type this because
he never was seriously hurt.) When we stopped laughing,
we ran below to check him out. We had to revive him and
saw he was only bruised and we all started laughing again.
That was the last time he played football with us. He switched
to basketball after that episode.

When the ship arrived into Norfolk, we would stay a
few weeks and then go out again to other ports. We went
to Algiers, England, France, Cuba, Greece, Italy, Jamaica,
Spain, Turkey, the Virgin Islands and many other places
that I can't recall at this moment. I must say I got to places
I never would have seen if I hadn't joined the Navy. Thanks,
Skippy.

So many things have happened to me, people kept saying, "I don't believe it." But this was the beginning . . . I was only nineteen years old. When I got on the Siboney, my first ship, I expected to get into the electrical shack, which seemed like a pretty good job, and the logical thing, being I had just come from electrical school. But this wasn't the logical way; this was the Navy way, so I was assigned to the boiler room. They said the electrical shack was filled at this time, but I would be transferred as soon as there was an opening. Little did I know that I would never leave the boiler room.

Now, you talk about terrible jobs: We would lie on the flight deck on our off-hours and get a beautiful tan, then go to work in the boiler room in 140-degree heat and lose our tan. We ended up with whitish-brown-colored skin. Everyone knew who worked in the boiler room just by looking at us.

A funny thing happened when I first got there. (I thought it was funny, anyway.) I was watching the water in the boiler while we were on a "speed run." My position was on the second level and I had been there about two hours while I watched the water level, which was about halfway on the glass. All of a sudden the ship made an abrupt stop and I could see everyone scurrying around below yelling, "Low water, low water." Wow, this never happened to me before. I didn't know what to do. Finally a Petty Officer came up to me and yelled, "Where's your water?"

I said, "It's in that little glass tube over there, I guess." We both walked over to the glass and it was empty. There was a crack in the glass that went right across it that made it look like the water line. It was the same line that was there when I relieved the guy before me but unfortunately for me, I got stuck with the low water. Anyway, I was right. The line never moved.

Well, as I stated, we were on a speed run, and the ship had to be stopped and the boiler had to be opened and checked inside. The funniest thing happened. The Division Officer had to get in an asbestos suit, after the boiler was shut down, and check the pipes inside to make sure there was no damage. After a few minutes he came running out. His asbestos suit, which isn't supposed to burn, was actually on fire; they had to extinguish the flames. It sure was funny watching this guy run out like that, but I was sure glad he wasn't injured. They might have blamed me. Actually, it was the Petty Officer's responsibility. Hey, I was an electrician, not a boiler man, and the lights were still working. I tried to tell them that in the beginning, that I was an electrician, but no one would listen. Maybe now they'll listen. (But they didn't.) They also said this was the first time one of these asbestos suits actually burned. I wonder if there was a "no burning clause" in effect. One guy said, "I don't believe it, I've never seen one of those suits burning before." I wanted to chip in and say believe it—I'm here and it's not over yet—but I didn't.

The only thing that kept most of us going in the boiler room was the spare time we had. We would either spend it on the flight deck or "work out." It was kind of like prison. We were confined and everybody worked out. The only thing missing was prison bars. That's all there was to do, and we did plenty of it. I was in great shape then and also continued boxing. I had gotten my amateur boxing license while I was in high school, after I quit basketball. I was boxing so much that I actually was thinking about a professional boxing career. Some of the guys that I was boxing were pros and some were much older than me, and if I beat them, I would think, hey, this is pretty easy. I might as well make some money at it. Fortunately, the girl I was going with at the time talked me out of it. That's the only good thing she did for me.

She was in the Air Force and was stationed at Andrews Air Force Base in Washington, D.C. This one weekend I surprised her and went to where she was staying, and caught her in the back seat of her car with a Marine. (Neither one was driving and that car was really moving.) I didn't realize it at the time, but that Marine did me a great favor. I wouldn't have ended up where I am today with a wonderful wife, kids and grandkids. She and I had been going together all through high school and were considering getting married when I got out of the service. I did go to her sister's wedding and that's where I met my wife, Madeline Tobin, who was a friend of her sister. So I guess my old girlfriend did do something good thing for me. Thanks.

After a few months in the boiler room, I got into the oil shack, which was a premier job within the boiler room. I think the Chief Petty Officer, who I helped with exercises in the workout room, had a hand in that. He was a great guy but I wonder if he was sorry he helped me, after a couple of oil incidents. The oil king's job was responsible for taking and removing oil to other ships, to move oil and water into different tanks and to keep the ship on an even keel. Actually, when you take on oil there are about thirty to forty valves that physically have to be checked before you start. Now, the guys who trained me said, "You really don't have to check them all because the last guy in front of you was supposed to have done it." Sounds pretty crazy but that's how they did it. I can honestly say that whenever I completed a job, I checked every valve and made sure it was closed. No one ever followed me and pumped oil over. Well, I wish I could say the same for everyone in front of me. Now, I'm not trying to put the blame on someone else, because I still was supposed to check before I started.

One such case was when we were refueling at the Marine base just outside Cherry Point, North Carolina. We took oil in on the port side and it went right out the starboard side. Before it was discovered, the beach at Cherry Point became flooded with oil. The poor bathers had to be removed and the beach was closed down for some time. Would you believe it? The Captain of our ship wanted to see the "Duty Oil King" personally. Now, most guys never get to see their Captains, let alone speak to them, their entire careers, and here I was with about a year in the service, and I'm doing both. Pretty

Impressive. Of course the only thing I said was 'yes, sir,' but I think I might have said it twice. He did all the talking. I don't think I'll ever forget that meeting. I have a funny feeling he might not either.

There were a few other incidents but not quite as severe. In fact, they didn't just happen to me. They even happened to the Chief Petty Officer. Like everyone else, he didn't check one valve and sure enough, we got a small spill. He asked me if I would take the responsibility for it because it wouldn't look as bad if a fireman had done it. Of course I took the blame. What are friends for?

One other incident sticks in my mind, because the Chief Petty Officer said this was a first. We were in the eye of a hurricane. We even had to eat sandwiches on the deck. When we ate, it was like the old Italian football weddings: everyone's throwing sandwiches around.

This is an extremely difficult time for the "Duty Oil King" and of course I was the duty oil king—a twenty-year-old kid; all these "old salts" conking out somewhere and I get stuck with the duty.

Maybe now you're starting to believe some of my stories. Maybe you're even beginning to feel a little sorry for me.

Well anyway, the ship was on an eighteen-degree list and I was pumping back and forth like crazy in an attempt to reduce the list. The Chief told me if we didn't reduce the list we would probably tip over. That was quite a list for an aircraft carrier. How's that for pressure on a twenty-year-old kid electrician working in the boiler room? The other "old salt" oil kings were actually making bets, some saying they thought I would tip the ship over. If I did, they would never be able to collect on their bets. Hey, some of those oil kings were on the ship for years and never had to handle a hurricane, let alone speak to the Captain. I had the opportunity to do both.

Finally, with some help from the Chief, we were able to get it under control. Hey, this time, the same Captain commended us for doing a good job. (I don't think he recognized me.) Still, the only thing I said was, 'yes, sir.' This time I only said it once.

My Chief actually saved me one time from getting in real trouble. I was just a fireman but when we took on oil, I was usually in charge of all the other firemen because I was an oil king. I had directed another fireman to move some hoses and he refused to do it. He said, "I'm a fireman just like you and I'm not taking orders from you." He just stood there in front of me, not moving, holding his hands on his hips and daring me to take some action. Well, remember, I had been boxing and had developed quite a good right hand. We called it my "Sleeper Punch." I let him have it in the solar plexus very hard. He went down and was out like a light. I left him there and we continued moving the hoses.

The Chief came over and saw him on the ground and asked me what happened. I nonchalantly told him he got hit by one of the hoses and just kept on working. They called the sick bay and brought him down there on a stretcher. A few minutes later the Chief came over to me and again asked me what happened. I then told him the truth. He said, "He should have listened to you. I put you in charge and that was like defying my orders." I fully agreed with him.

The problem was the Division Officer was going down to sick bay to check the man out who was hit by the oil hose. The Chief and I quickly went down to sick bay. The man was now conscious and telling everyone that I hit him. The Chief talked very sternly to him and said, "Listen, if you want to stay in this man's Navy and work for me, you got hit by the hose—do you understand that? This man was acting for me and I would have belted you too." Amazingly, when the Division Officer came down for the story, the fireman told him it was an accident, and he had been injured by the hose. Another irony: apparently some bones had been broken by the punch and because he didn't have much time left, they gave him a medical discharge.

Would you believe before he left the ship, he actually thanked me. "Anytime," I said. "Glad I was able to help."

Once I made Third-Class Petty Officer, I was able to work shore patrol. I loved it. We would go out into the town, armed with nightsticks. All we really did was fight drunken sailors and Marines. At that time I was in such good shape, I never had any problems. In Kingston, Jamaica we worked with the police in convertibles. This sealed it for me. I would become a policeman. Where else could you fight and not get in trouble—and ride in convertibles, and get paid for it?

One incident does stick in my mind. Another sailor and I were patrolling outside some bars in the Virgin Islands. About ten obnoxious, drunken sailors came out of the bar; we went over towards them to quiet them down. All of a sudden about six of them jumped me, and started flailing away. From the corner of my eye I could see my partner running away. I couldn't believe it. Now they were all on me, really punching away. They worked me over pretty well. My white uniform was all bloody (mostly mine) and ripped. After getting their rips in, they left me and took off.

I was finally able to get up. I couldn't believe I didn't have any broken bones, but I was bruised all over. By the time I got to the ship, I was really mad. Near the front gangplank, I observed my partner coming towards me. He looked so nice and clean in his white uniform. He started to tell me he was going for help. That was the last word I heard him say, "help." I went at him with both fists. I hit him like I was hitting the punching bag. The only difference is this felt much, much better. I think I did hear him say "help" again but it was too late now to help him. When I left him on the ground he looked worse than me.

Just then our Chief came by and looked at both of us. "What the hell happened to you guys?" he asked.

"We got jumped by ten sailors, Chief." He just laughed

and walked away. I made sure I never had that partner again, and I didn't.

A funny thing occurred with that same Chief. I had shore patrol a few days after that and he was coming back from liberty, and heading for the boat to take him back to the carrier. I was on the pier and he came over to me and was obviously inebriated. He used to box with me once in a while, and he immediately started swinging at me, stating, "Come on, Natch, I can take you."

Now I know he was playfully doing this but he was swinging pretty hard. I said, "Come on, Chief, just get into the boat, please."

Of course he paid no attention to me, getting closer to me as I was sidestepping him. Eventually he took a big swing and I jumped to the side as he went over the edge of the pier and fell into the boat below, flat on his face. Ow, it hurt just watching him land on the hard surface. Again, I'm starting to laugh as I type this because I can picture this in my mind even though it happened many years ago. He just about knocked himself out, but he really wasn't hurt, except for a few lumps and bruises.

I didn't know what to expect from him the next day, when I had to work for him. Believe it or not he never said a word about it, ever. I think he really didn't remember it. He was quite a guy, we got along great. I really respected him and I'm glad he forgot.

Now here's some irony. His name was Smith. The policeman on the beat by my parents' store who was so influential to me was Smith, and the first Sergeant that I worked with on the job was Smith. One more thing: believe it or not, one of my best buddies on the Siboney was a Smith. My life was full of Smiths. Oh yes, I almost forgot this: One of my wife's best friends is Jean Smith, who was our neighbor on Chestnut Street for a while. She was one of the ones I fingerprinted for practice, when I was learning how. And believe this or not, the first guy I arrested for burglary, I got through his fingerprints (he went for thirteen jobs), and he was a Smith. I guess you could say I had good and bad Smith relationships.

One other Navy story I must tell is when we were in Algiers. Now, everyone has heard about the "Casbah." This was an area of Algiers where "anything goes." There's no law or restrictions there. Now you know we had to go there. Of course, they wouldn't allow military personnel there, so we went to a shop and bought some Arab robes and rolled up our pants and proceeded to the Casbah. We had to sneak by the shore patrol and military police who were stationed in front to keep guys like us out.

Well, you can imagine six sailors traveling in an unknown area, looking for some action. It wasn't long before we got it. We were easily spotted. Most of the garb we had on didn't fit us and our white navy pants were hanging below our robes. We were really a funny sight to see, but not to a bunch of young Arabs, who started towards us. All I could see were the two-foot-long bolo knives they were swinging and waving. I yelled to the others, "I think it's time to run." Boy, did we. We ran right out of the Casbah and into a jeep with MPs sitting just outside. They were stationed there to keep military people like us from going in. We had walked right by them going in. We dropped our robes and went to the jeep. They escorted us to safety. That was the end of the Casbah for us.

The rest of my time in the Navy was very uneventual except for a few "You wouldn't believe it" stories, some of which I can't print.

I served on the Midway, the Valley Forge and the Sibony. The Midway was the largest carrier at the time and had over 3,000 men aboard it. I was only there about six months and was getting transferred to the Valley Forge. As I was leaving, my supervisor, an old-salt First-Class Petty Officer, came to the gangplank to see me off. I had a couple of little oil spills while I was there, so he called me "Overs." He said as I was leaving, "Overs, you were on this ship less than a year and I want you to know, some guys have worked for me for over ten years and I've forgotten them. But you, I'll never forget." I'm still trying to figure out if this was a compliment or what.

Well, I think I'll take it as a compliment. I can use them.

I was honorably discharged as a boiler man, Third-Class Petty Officer, June 10, 1955. At the time I was going with a woman named Hazel. Hazel was a bit older than me and had three children by a previous husband, so I didn't go home. I stayed at Hazel's house. Fortunately I sent most of my money home and bought a one-way bus ticket to Newark. I figured when my money ran out I would go home. Hazel had different ideas. She wanted to get married. She really was a nice person and the kids were great too, but I wasn't really ready yet. Besides, I was only twenty-three years old and she was thirty-one. When my money ran out, I did leave. I told Hazel I would be back but I knew I wouldn't be.

When I got to Newark (with the ticket I had bought and stuck in my wallet), I didn't have one penny, not even a dime for a telephone call. I had to hitchhike home at three AM. When I told my mother and my sister about Hazel, they both persuaded me not to go back. So I didn't. I got a call from Hazel about one month later and she asked me if I was coming back and I told her I wasn't. I found out she later married an old buddy of mine from the ship and again I wasn't invited to the wedding. (This happens to me all the time.)

A couple of weeks after I got home I went back to work for Bob Frei, the electrician who I worked for before the Navy. One note about the Navy, only because it just came up a few years ago. It's hard to believe but I never really learned how to swim in the Navy. Thank God the ship never went down.

We had a pool in our back yard for years (a four-foot-deep pool). I taught all three of my kids how to swim. I always had one leg on the bottom and they thought I was actually swimming. They couldn't believe I was in the Navy and never knew how to swim. You probably wonder how I got away with not learning how to swim in the Navy. Let me explain this reality. When they tested us, they used a large bamboo pole and kept moving it up a little at a time. I just kept hanging on to the pole and pulling myself along. They never really paid much attention and assumed I was swimming. Well, I wasn't. I was just hanging on for dear life. When I got to the end they just said, "Next." Well, I guess that was the Navy way.

In fact, no one in my family knew I couldn't swim until just recently. Our family all went out in my-son-in-law Pat's boat at Lake George. Of course, we all wore life jackets, so I was covered. We came to a high cliff that all my grandkids and the rest of the family all jump from. How could I not jump? Hey, I had a life jacket on. When I was about to jump, someone from a boat nearby told me not to jump with the life jacket on because I could choke myself. Well, I didn't take the life jacket off and I didn't jump from that cliff but from the next cliff down, which was about fifteen feet high. I also held the life jacket tightly around my neck so it wouldn't move much. Well, it hurt a little but it was better than drowning.

Anyway, my whole family now knows I can't swim. The first thing my son-in-law Pat said to his wife was, "LeeAnn, did you know your father can't swim?" She said, "I don't believe it. He taught me how to swim!"

CHAPTER 6

JOINING THE POLICE DEPARTMENT

IN FEBRUARY OF 1956, I took the Montclair Police exam and was appointed a probationary patrolman. I was assigned to the Police Academy in Cedar Grove and did quite well. I had a 94.8 average and just missed winning the weapon that the student with the highest average gets. The number-one recruit had 95-point-something—I don't remember but I know it was less than a point beyond my mark.

I was then assigned to a "walking beat" on the Montclair Police Department and once in a while worked in the radio car. I loved it but I sure didn't like the cold winter nights. Whenever it got really cold, I swore I would quit.

I think I was on the job only a few days when I realized I was going to have some problems with this one Sergeant who was conducting an inspection of our weapons before we went on duty. When I pulled mine out and opened the cylinder, I must have had it upside-down because all the bullets fell out and hit the floor. All the guys in the line-up started scrambling around to get out of the way. You would think they would know that bullets hitting the ground couldn't explode. (At least that's what I thought.) Well, they didn't explode so I must have been right. Needless to say, after that, the Sergeant watched me very closely.

I was only on the job a couple of months when I got some action. I was walking the beat at the corner of Bloomfield Avenue and Grove Street. I observed a car stopped at the traffic light heading east. I still remember the plate number: KE8; it was the Mayor of Woodbridge's auto and, according to the teletype I read before I came on duty, it had been stolen about a week prior. I knew this wasn't just kids joyriding. I slowly approached the auto to get in a position to stop it. Just as I got near the door they spotted me and took off, going through the red light, heading east.

I immediately commandeered the next car in line and instructed the driver to "follow that car." Now, there were two men in the front and two woman in the back seat. The stolen car was really going at a great rate of speed and the driver of the car I was in was very reluctant to get close to it. I kept telling him to speed it up and I can now understand why he was reluctant to do it.

As we got into Glen Ridge and near Ridgewood Avenue, I reached out the window and fired my weapon in the air. We had no radios at this time and I thought that if I fired my weapon there, the Glen Ridge Police might hear me and respond. At this time the women in the back were quite excited and kept yelling, "Oh boy, just like television." One said, "Are you trying to shoot the tire, Officer?" I didn't answer her . . . of course I was.

Unfortunately, the Glen Ridge Police didn't respond. At the next traffic light, the stolen auto went around all the cars stopped at the light and into oncoming traffic; fortunately there wasn't too much. My driver did the same but going much slower. He continued on to Glenwood Avenue at Bloomfield Center and made a right heading towards East Orange. My driver wouldn't go around these cars so I quickly jumped out and ran towards the Center, knowing there is usually a police car around there. Sure enough, there was a police car sitting just off of the Center. I don't know how he didn't see or hear the auto going around all those cars and through the red light, but he obviously didn't. I was about one minute behind the stolen auto, so I jumped into the police car, nearly scaring the Lieutenant sitting in it half to death.

Very excitedly I told the Lieutenant to hurry up and turn around because I was just chasing this stolen auto that just sped by him. You're not going to believe this, but he started asking me questions about the car. I said, "Please, Lieutenant, just turn the car around and head in that direction and I'll give you all the info."

He said, "Just calm down, kid, and give me the plate number."

I pleaded with him to chase them as I gave him the plate number. He didn't move. Maybe three minutes later the plate I gave him came back over his radio and confirmed that it was stolen. He then slowly started to turn around in the direction the stolen auto went and said to me, "Relax, kid, if we don't catch them they'll get caught."

I then told the Lieutenant to turn his car around and take me back to Montclair . . . which he did. All the way back he was trying to pacify me but I wouldn't let him off the hook. It's probably the first time a "rookie" had admonished a Lieutenant but I sure did . . . all the way back to Montclair.

By the way, this same group committed a hold-up and

robbery, wounding the victim, a few days later. I wanted to call up that Lieutenant and tell him—but I didn't.

Another weird incident occurred when I worked the Fourth Ward Downtown. Now, most of the people there were Italians so I shouldn't have had any problems, right? Wrong. I guess I was a little strict because I did give a lot of tickets, especially around the Clubs. Hey, I figured if you had enough money to gamble, you had enough money to pay for your tickets. Well, as a result I wasn't too popular in that area.

This one day I was giving a car a ticket on "No Parking This Side." While I was putting it on the windshield, the driver came out and started yelling at me. I told him to take the ticket and leave. He grabbed the ticket from my hand and then pushed me. I grabbed him and spun him around and attempted to handcuff him. He was quite big and we tussled a little. I finally got him on the ground and held my nightstick under his neck so he couldn't move. By this time a large crowd had gathered. We didn't have radios then, so I asked one of the people nearby to call police headquarters. No one complied. In fact, they all started to walk away. It seemed like no one was going to call for me.

A young woman was still nearby and I yelled to her to call the police. She walked away and I wasn't sure if she would or not, but within minutes I heard a siren and not long after two radio cars arrived. We brought him to headquarters and arrested him. I found out the woman had called for me. When I got back to the post I looked for the woman to thank her, but couldn't find her.

I was off the next two days and when I came back to the same post, I heard we had a murder on the post while I was off. When I checked it further, I discovered it was the young woman who had called the police for me. It had nothing to do with her helping me, thank goodness. It seemed that she was a prostitute, and an elderly gentleman from the area was living with her and hadn't known about her profession. He found out and went completely berserk. A butcher by trade, he stabbed her to death, then cut her up into little pieces like he was fileting a side of beef. He then put the pieces in garbage bags and placed her with the garbage for pickup at the curb. It wasn't long before she was found. It also wasn't long before detectives working the case found the ex-butcher and arrested him.

Another irony . . . this same man had been arrested many years earlier on a previous murder and was on parole.

My first big dangerous encounter came while I was going to work on the midnight shift. I was in my own car, traveling south on Midland Avenue, and as I approached Claremont Avenue, I saw a car going very slowly traveling west. As I got closer I saw a man reaching into the driver's side with both hands inside the vehicle, which was stopped for a red light. It appeared as if he was choking the driver. The driver was slumped in the seat.

I stopped my car in front of the car and ran out towards it. I shouted, "Stop, Police!" The man who was reaching in saw me and let go of the victim. He started to run north on Midland Avenue. I was about six to eight feet behind him. He ran into the bushes at the side of a house on Midland Avenue where I could no longer see him, because it was too dark. I had my weapon out and proceeded towards the bushes. I couldn't see him but he could obviously see me because there was a street light behind me. Suddenly I felt him on top of me, knocking me to the ground. I was still in pretty good shape but this guy was strong as an ox. He grabbed my gun hand and I could feel him groping for the trigger. I tried to turn it towards him but with his strength I could feel the gun barrel dig into my stomach. The gun was in my left hand and with all my strength, and my right hand, I grabbed the barrel of the gun and twisted it towards him. He then pulled the trigger and would you believe it? He shot himself. I could feel the heat of the bullet on my hand as he fell to the ground.

I stood up and started towards the house to get help. He

suddenly jumped up and started running into the bushes. I immediately tackled him and held him down.

This alley that it occurred in was the driveway of a police officer I worked with, Patrolman Dominick Valente, who was getting ready to go to work. He heard the shot and called for assistance. A radio car arrived and we drove the suspect to the hospital. Apparently he had a stomach wound but it wasn't too serious.

To our surprise, the victim he was choking was already there. They were performing an emergency operation to open up his throat. The passenger in his car had immediately driven him to the hospital. If it weren't for him, I would have been involved in my first homicide.

Now I'm going to go a little further in time, only because it involves this same guy. He was charged with attempted murder, assault and battery, and violation of probation and put in Trenton State Prison. A few years later this guy escaped from prison and a few days after that he was spotted in Montclair on Bloomfield Avenue. Somehow he eluded about eight policemen with them firing numerous shots at him. It's really too bad none hit their mark because the next day he held up a small store in East Orange, killing the owner and seriously wounding his wife.

Anyway, the next day he was again spotted in Montclair, this time during the day, and I was working in the Detective Bureau and heard the call. I told the other detective to drive because I was going to be the "runner." We got to the area where he was seen and I immediately spotted him at Lackawanna Plaza. I jumped out of the car and was on him so fast, he never saw me until I had the gun up against his head. He had a very large knife under his belt, which he never got to; we cuffed him and brought him to headquarters.

It was only then that I learned that he kept coming back to Montclair to look for me and kill me because I had arrested him on the earlier charge. He also told us that the guy he was choking on the earlier arrest had also got him arrested and that's why he was trying to get him. The ironic thing was this guy would wait in the bushes and hope the guy (that he was choking) would get the red light at that intersection so he could jump out and get him while the car was stopped. This is an amazing string of events, especially considering that the light had to be red, and I came by in my private car at that same time. Even more strange was that I never usually came to work that way.

As you will see, a lot of strange things happened to me or around me. There are things that I am going to put in this book that you would never put in a book because who would believe it? Well hey, that's the name of this book. It could have no other name.

To go back to where I was in this original story, I was still a patrolman and I think a very conscientious one. When I worked midnights, on my break, I would grab a sandwich and coffee, usually about three AM, find an empty milk box and go behind the stores, sit down and watch the area while I ate and had my coffee.

This one time the radio car pulled up to me and had their coffee, and my old buddy Skippy was in the car. That's right, the same one who got me in the Navy. (I did him the same favor. I talked him into joining the police department.) He was on the adjoining post. So we all sat in the radio car very quietly and were drinking our coffee. We were parked just off of the street and in the driveway of a lumberyard. As we were drinking our coffee, we spotted four guys creeping into the lumberyard from the other side of the driveway. We waited (they couldn't see us) until one of them actually started forcing the side door. We immediately got out and grabbed each one of them. Boy, were they surprised. All were charged with breaking and entering. This one was really easy. The only problem was, when it happened this way, we would have to throw out our coffee, but it was worth it.

One of the most dangerous types of calls is the Family Disturbance. Sometimes you would go there and try and separate husband and wife and they both end up beating on you. This happened so many times . . . almost daily. One time I do remember because this guy was so strong he actually broke the handcuffs. There were four pretty big guys on this call: Joe Harrington, Cokey DeNicola, Skippy Rizzie, and I was the smallest, at 210 pounds. When he broke the handcuffs we couldn't believe it, but we all jumped right in again and were finally able to subdue him. This time we put two pairs of cuffs on him and they held. Prior to us getting there, he threw his three-month-old baby across the room and against the wall. Miraculously, the baby wasn't injured too badly.

Before I continue with the next part, I want to say this. Most of all policemen are honest hard-working people, but some do stray off. The police job, probably more than any other, has the most temptations. Now if you're not completely honest, you could have problems. The other problem is some are honest but won't squeal on the ones who were not.

We used to check store doors during the night. I would find one open and call it in. Soon, other officers would arrive and help you check it out. It didn't take me long to find out who the ones were who were not so honest. I immediately let them all know where I stood. This, believe it or not, got me in trouble with some of the honest cops. When they came after I found a door open I told them, "Anyone who takes anything is under arrest." Some of them laughed at this but wouldn't take anything in front of me. One older Sergeant, who wouldn't take anything, came up to me and said, "Hey kid, it's been going on for years, you can't stop it."

I said, "Sergeant, you're just as guilty as them for allowing it."

Well, this really got around and the word was "Don't trust Naturale." That was fine with me. At least they knew where I stood and they would never do it around me.

One time during a midnight shift I watched one of the guys that I was sure wasn't completely honest. I put a pebble on the trunk of his private car. The pebble was gone each time I checked it. I put five pebbles on during the night, meaning he opened his trunk at least five times. Now you don't have to be Einstein to figure what he was doing. After the shift he went over to his trunk with another patrolman and opened it and gave him a couple of bags from the trunk. As I neared them they immediately threw them back into the trunk and shut it.

I saw the Uniform Supervisor a little later and advised him of what had occurred. He somewhat pacified me, stating, "Oh, that could have been anything." Well, I knew where I stood with him now. In fact, a couple of days later I was transferred to the uptown beat away from the two patrolmen.

Not long after that I was riding with another patrolman who apparently hadn't heard about me yet. We found a store open on Grove Street and while I was checking the front, he was emptying out the back. Now I was driving and I had the keys, so when I saw this I yelled to him to return the stuff or the car wasn't moving. He said, "Come on, I got some for you too. Let's get out of here, the Sergeant's on his way."

I told him the car wasn't moving until he returned everything. He very reluctantly put it all back. Just as he got it all back, the Sergeant arrived. I said to the patrolman, "If you ever do that again in front of me, I'll arrest you."

The next day he went to that same supervisor and said he didn't want to ride with me again. That was fine with me. I guess that's why I was made the first Internal Affairs Officer that Montclair ever had . . . but we're not there yet. I'm still a patrolman.

While I was a walking patrolman, many incidents occurred. The same Sergeant who said I couldn't change things was really on my back. I would walk all night while some guys slept in the cars. One night while a radio officer was napping in the driveway of Hillside School, I was walking around. I was actually doing pull-ups on the goalposts, which were a few feet away. I was actually up in the air when he pulled up with his bright lights on me. He jumped out of the car and started yelling at me, "Hey, Naturale, you should be walking your post, not hanging on the goalpost!"

I quickly jumped down and got just as angry with him. I yelled, "Would you rather me sleep in the car, like your friend over there?" He just walked away, never saying a word to the patrolman in the car who, by now, was awake, after all the shouting.

Another night he was watching me very closely. I purposely was walking very slowly on Bloomfield Avenue and could see his reflection in the passing plate glass windows, near St. Luke's Place. It was now about 4:13 AM, and the Sergeant knew I had a box ring at 4:15 AM at North Willow Street and Bloomfield Avenue . . . quite a few blocks away. Now, if you didn't make these rings on time, you usually got booked (written up). I guess he figured he had me because he turned around before he reached me and shot down the avenue to North Willow Street and Bloomfield Avenue, where the box was located. As soon as he turned, I turned it on; I ran down Bloomfield Avenue, across the town lot, through the Crescent lot, through the Wellmont Theater lot and then slowly walked across Bloomfield Avenue. I looked at my watch; I had about fifteen seconds before 4:15 AM. I got to the box and made my call . . . as the Sergeant, who was waiting a few feet from the box, approached me.

I said, "Hi, Sergeant, what's up?"

I knew he was more than angry as I stared right into his beet-red face. He then said, "Where's your car? I know you have your car with you on the post."

Calmly I said, "Why no, Sergeant, why do you say that?"

He was really stammering by now, saying, "But, but, but . . . I just saw you at St. Luke's Place, at the top of the hill."

"I know, Sergeant, I saw you too, but I'm a very fast walker."

Livid, beyond communication, he just sped off and I didn't see him for the rest of the tour. Until the day he retired he swore I had a car. After that I really played with him. I would climb to the top of high buildings, either through the fire escape or through hallway doors that sometimes were left open. From the roofs of the high buildings I could see all over town. I could actually see his car patrolling the streets, usually looking for me. I had a small pair of binoculars that I kept with me at all times; I could see him coming and would pop out in front of him, usually scaring him almost to death. When he would ask where I was, I would take my little pad out and read off all the places I had seen him. I would say, "I saw you, Sergeant, didn't you see me?" Eventually he stopped bothering me and let me do my job.

Once I really irked him. He was working the desk. It was about 7:30 AM and I brought in an inebriated guy and arrested him. Now, he was just getting ready to leave after the guy was put in the cell and I said, "Sergeant, you can't leave yet, someone's posting his twenty-five-dollar bail."

"Where are they? I don't see anyone with bail."

I looked him straight in the eye, with a twenty and a five in my hand, and said, "Here's the bail. I'm posting it, Sergeant, now let him out."

"Come on, Natch, you arrested him, you can't do that."

"So is it against the law for me to bail out my prisoner? See you tomorrow night, Sergeant, I'm leaving."

Finally, there was an incident that really broke the ice for us when this really funny thing happened to me and he was working that night. While I was checking the Bellevue Theater, I found the door open. Well, I started looking around and found the projection door open also. Now this door led to the roof and I had never been on the theater roof before, so I stepped out on it. Unfortunately, this was a slate roof and a little wet, and as I stepped out on it, I slipped. This was a very slanted roof and I couldn't stop myself and I kept sliding down, thinking I would at least break both my legs. As I got to the end of the roof

I grabbed at the letters that were sticking up. I was able to stop my fall by hanging on between two letters, but I couldn't move without me dropping down. Now it was about four AM and I didn't know how long I could hang on. And then, you'll never believe it: my favorite Sergeant pulled up in front of the theater. He was shining his light into the theater, probably looking for me. I never thought I'd be glad to see this Sergeant.

Well, anyway, he kept shining his light in the theater and I yelled, "Sergeant, up here."

He said, "Where the hell are you?" He kept looking in the theater.

Finally I said, "Look up between the B and E at the top of the theater."

Believe it or not, he started laughing and was just about rolling around on the pavement. He yelled, "What's the matter, Batman, are you stuck?" When he finally stopped laughing, he went over to the fire department around the corner and came with a big ladder and helped me down.

After that incident he always referred to me as "Batman." We also got along much better after that. He always knew I wouldn't be sleeping on the midnight shift but never knew on top of what building he would find me. I was so glad we ended it on a good note because not too long after that he retired, took a job as a bank guard, and was shot and killed in a hold-up shortly after getting the job.

Another odd incident occurred (which I thought was funny) when I was in the radio car not long after that incident. My partner and I had chased a car at a high rate of speed into Verona. The driver just wouldn't stop and kept going right into the driveway of his home, off of Route 23. We pulled up in front of the house, chased him as he ran from his car attempting to get into his house. We caught him before he got there, placed him under arrest and brought him to our patrol car. My partner got behind the wheel to drive as I was getting into the back with the prisoner. I cuffed him and put him in the back seat.

Somehow, with his hands, he was able to open the opposite door and exit. I followed right out the same door and he started running again and I again was chasing him. Talk about "Keystone Kops," this was it.

My partner never knew we both went in and out of the car and he went driving down the street with both doors wide open, oblivious to what had occurred. He finally realized it and came back and found me on top of the suspect in the middle of the street. It seems funnier now because we did catch him and eventually booked him. He was highly inebriated at the time, and later stated he didn't remember anything. I remember it well, forty years later. Oh well, all's well that ends well.

Unfortunately, this patrolman wasn't too honest. He was working part time in a confectionery store on Bloomfield Avenue many years later while I was the Internal Affairs Officer. I met with the owner and we set up his register with marked bills. Later that night when we checked it, the bills had been removed. The patrolman was searched and he had the bills on him. He was never actually charged but was immediately fired from the Police Department, to the satisfaction of the owner.

Our wedding at The Well on November 10, 1956, in Caldwell, NJ. L to R: Me, my bride and best man: Donald Stake

L to R: Donald and Dottie Stake, me and Charles Fergus and my sister Madie.

My bride and I, November 10, 1956.

Peggy Rutan (Habermann) catches the bouquet at our
wedding.

CHAPTER 7

MY MOTHER AND FATHER

THERE WERE MANY humorous incidents on the job and quite a few involved my mother. Now anyone who knew her would understand them because she was more like "Gracie Allen" than Gracie Allen.

This incident occurred when she pulled out from our family-owned business, Ace Cleaners, and started driving up Bloomfield Avenue. When she got in front of the Wellmont Theater, some packages fell from the front seat onto the floor of the car. She just reached over and bent down to pick them up at the same time the police officer directing traffic came into the middle of the street to stop traffic. All he saw was a driver-less car coming directly toward him. Fortunately, he was able to jump back, just enough so the vehicle didn't hit him. He immediately furiously started blowing his whistle. He then saw her head rise; she, too, must have heard the whistle because she stopped a few feet further down the road. Now this is the really funny part . . . as the officer later told me. She started crying and proceeded to tell him her whole life story and she ended up with, "And you must know my son, he's a police officer and he works with you." He said she just kept talking and talking and traffic was backing up. He finally said, "Mrs. Naturale, please leave. You are free to go . . . please!"

The next day the officer related this story to me and asked me, "How's your ill grandmother doing?"

Concerned, I said, "Why?"

He said, "Your mother told me she is dying and that's why she was so preoccupied and didn't see me in the middle of the street."

I said, "Oh, she's much better now." Grandma Caroline was healthier than me.

Another Mom story. It was about five PM and we had just received information about a holdup in the area involving four young men. I observed four men fitting the description we were given at the corner of North Willow Street and Bloomfield Avenue. I stopped them, at gunpoint, and had them lined up against the Willow Bar wall. I held them there and slowly backed into the street, heading to the call box on the corner just a few feet away. As I was slowly backing onto the street, and still closely observing the suspects, a speeding car came careening around the corner, almost running over my feet. I jumped backwards to avoid being hit. The car stopped right in front of me; it was my mother! Of course I'm still holding my weapon . . . she looked at it . . . then at me . . . and yelled, "Anthony, what are you doing with that gun?" Of course I reminded her I'm a policeman. She then yelled, "Will you put that thing away before you get hurt!" Now I'm even getting snickering from the suspects as they turned to see what the commotion was all about. One quietly said, "It's his mother!"

After a short time my mother began to understand the situation and even asked if she could help me. "Ma, just leave, please!" Finally she left and I got to the box to call for assistance so we could thoroughly check the perpetrators out for identification.

It turned out they weren't the holdup men. So I

approached them, telling them I was sorry for the inconvenience. They were very understanding. Before they left, one of them came up to me and said, "Officer, was that lady really your mother? That is the funniest thing I've seen in a long time." I would see this guy over the years and we became quite friendly; he even used to go into our cleaners and talk to my mother as they became good friends and always used to chuckle about the incident. He was a good customer of theirs for many years.

My mother was always at the wrong place at the wrong time. One morning she went into the Shop-Rite grocery store on Grove Street at about ten AM. As she was passing through the front door, a man pushed her from behind, sticking something into her back with a blanket over the object. The object turned out to be a shotgun. He pushed her through the front door and into the store with two armed men alongside of him. My mother started screaming and yelling so much (she's very excitable) that they made her go into the standup freezer, along with the manager and the other customers, and get on the floor face-down. They first had them empty their pockets and handbags, taking whatever valuables that there were. After a few minutes, they left.

Soon after the manager was able to unlock the freezer from the inside and called the police. He told everyone, "Come on out, the police are on their way!" Well, everyone complied except my mother. She told the manager, from her position on the floor, "I'm not moving until my son, 'the detective' comes." When I got there a few minutes later, the manager told me everyone was out of the freezer except one lady who wouldn't get off the floor until her son "the detective" arrived. Now there were about four detectives responding but I knew immediately it was my mother. I told the manager, "That's my mother! She thinks I'm Sherlock Holmes." I went into the freezer and there she was, just as they had left her, lying flat on the floor; she was half-frozen. When she saw me she jumped up and started telling me the story. Then she leaned over to me and very calmly said, "They didn't get my wallet with my money and baby pictures! When they had me lie down on the floor, I slipped my wallet out of my purse and threw it in the corner; they weren't going to get my grandkids' pictures!"

Well, believe it or not, a similar incident happened just a few months after. My mom was closing the cleaners about six PM, went to her car in the lot next door, was about to get into the car when a guy approached, grabbed her purse and attempted to run off with it. She had it wrapped around her shoulder and, when he grabbed it, she also grabbed it; he was pulling one way and she was pulling in the opposite direction. Don't ask me how she did it but somehow, with one hand, she slipped her wallet out, dropped it to the ground (she was getting good at this), let go of the purse and fell over backwards; he still had the purse in his hands so he got up and ran, thinking he got the loot. He got an empty purse with a lot of old envelopes. She would always write on envelopes and stick them in her pocketbook. The bad part was, because my mother wouldn't let go of the purse, she injured her shoulder and had to be taken to the hospital and be treated.

Now, some more irony: The night crew caught this guy and locked him up. I came in the next day working in the ID bureau and the Captain said, "Guess what, Tony? They caught the guy that injured your mother. Do you want to get him from the cell block and print him?"

Eagerly I said, "I would love to, Captain." So I did. Now I'm not a brutal person, and I never believed in 'police brutality,' but sometimes there are 'extenuating circumstances.' And this was one of them. This guy was about six-foot-six but a real thin drink of water. As I was printing him, I was asking him questions about the theft. I said, "Why did you hurt that woman that you took the purse from?"

He said, "She wouldn't give it up."

At this time I took him in the darkroom to take his

picture. As I was snapping the picture I said, "That woman you robbed and put in the hospital was my mother."

He said, "Oh, shit." If you looked at his mug shot today, I think you can see exactly what he's saying. That was the last word I heard him say because, as he stood straight up, I buried my right fist in his stomach. Now when I say I buried it, I mean it, because from boxing and working out on the bag almost daily, I developed quite a right hand. He hit the floor like a sack of potatoes and didn't move; he was out like a light. I opened the door and he sprawled across the doorway as I stepped over him.

The Captain, who was just a few feet away, never stopped typing. He just said, "You okay, Tony?"

Without skipping a beat I said, "I'm fine, Captain, thank you."

The perp woke up a couple of minutes later and told me he was sorry he hurt my mother. I saw him many more times, usually because I was processing him for another crime, but never any more against my mother. After that incident I was known as "Tough Tony" to some of my fellow workers.

My mom was involved in many incidents without me involved. As I said, she was always at the wrong place at the wrong time. One day, in the middle of heavy traffic, she pulled from the curb in front of the cleaners, right into the fast-moving traffic on Bloomfield Avenue. Somehow I think she thought the road was made just for her because, when she pulled into the lane, the car coming up directly behind her, to avoid hitting her, had to go into the opposite lane of traffic, which was also heavy. Now he collided head-on into the car coming down Bloomfield Avenue; the car directly behind this car stopped and the car behind *him* hit him as well as the car behind . . . oh well, let's just suffice it to say she caused a twelve-car accident. Cars were all over the place. Thank God there were no serious injuries. Of course my mother just rode off into the sunset, completely oblivious to what had just occurred. Now to hear my mother tell it she said,

"There was a big accident in front of the cleaners today!" Never believing she had anything to do with it. I tried to explain to her that she was the cause but she didn't believe me. She believed me when her insurance company had to pay for the damages.

Well, I could write a whole book on my mother and most people who knew her probably could as well.

She also got me started on the "Fitness Craze." She would listen to nutritionist Gaylord Hauser, and make all this crazy stuff. She's probably the only Italian who puts wheat germ in her meatballs. She would exercise constantly and she was jitterbugging with me on her seventy-sixth birthday; her grandkids called her "Meatball Gram." She was also known for her cream puffs (which she didn't put wheat germ in) and her pasta-fazool.

I was involved in an accident too. Like mother like son, I guess. I was coming to work in my own car proceeding north on Midland Avenue. At Walnut Street I stopped, being a good law-abiding policeman that I was, and started across the intersection. Suddenly I saw this car coming east on Walnut Street right in front of me. The best I could do was brake the car. But my front bumper caught the rear bumper of the car as it almost passed me, knocking it out of control. It continued on, striking a tree just to the left of me. I, in uniform, quickly ran from my car to the two passengers who were still in the front seats. I helped them both out of the car; I could hear the siren of the ambulance in the background. The car was pretty smashed up and both of them seemed to be shaken up but not hurt too badly. The man then remarked to his wife, "See, dear, the police are here . . . we'll be okay." Then he turned to me and said, "Officer, you guys do such a good job! You got here so fast." I didn't have the heart to tell him that it was me who hit him. Not at this, time anyway. Afterwards I saw him at the hospital and gave him all the information, including my license and registration. I still couldn't tell him because he was telling everyone how quickly the police responded and got them out of the car.

The fact is, I never told him; he must have thought that the license and registration I gave him was from the person who struck him. Well, he was right about that. We didn't have picture licenses then. That's why we have insurance. I let them handle it all the way. If he ever reads this book he'll be very surprised.

I haven't mentioned much about my father. That's because when my mother was around, she was always the one involved with everything. There are many moments I cherish of my father, but none so dear as the day he became a hero to me.

Early on I knew I had a wonderful mother and father, but I never saw enough of them as they worked all the time. Other kids seemed to be going places with their parents; not us. Now that we lived in Upper Montclair, my dad worked two jobs: in the cleaners during the day and then for another cleaners at night as a tailor. The only time we would all be together was on a Sunday.

Sunday was extra special, not only because we had our mother and father all day, but the delicious foods my mother would cook. She was an amazing cook, and although she worked all week, she would toil all day cooking and cleaning. Although I hated it at the time, my job was to clean the table after the meal. Madie washed the dishes and Junior would dry them. This one Sunday I remember my father saying, "Let's go, kids!" He was smiling from ear to ear as he loaded chicken cutlet and eggplant sandwiches into a big bag. "It's too hot to stay home! We're going to Lake Hiawatha and go swimming!" In those days there actually was a lake there.

We loaded the car with an inner tube, some blankets and towels and were on our way. I believe I was around eight years old, Madie had to be ten and little Junior was six.

We were good as gold as we traveled in the car what seemed to be a very long distance away. The three of us were sitting in the back singing, "Mares eat oats and does eat oats and little lambs eat ivy . . . a kid will eat ivy too . . . wouldn't you," and my mother and father actually joined in singing with us. It felt like we were on a holiday. To us, this was a big thing because we never really went many places because they both worked so much. We kids didn't appreciate them always working but I certainly understand the reasons now.

It seemed like it took forever to get there, and when we did, we jumped out of the car and couldn't wait to get to the lake. Daddy told us to stay close as we may get lost. All of a sudden, as we were crossing a small bridge, little Vic (Junior) teetered, slipped as he grabbed at air, and disappeared into over six feet of water. It happened so fast I just froze in my tracks. I stared, bug-eyed, as my father threw the bags he was holding to the ground and was in the lake so fast, he too disappeared; I could see him bobbing up and down. The sun seemed to disappear and then, suddenly, I saw him groping with his large hands for Junior. Dad popped up, raising Junior over his head. But my heart stopped because, although Junior was in the air, Dad was going down, then popping up again but getting closer to the bridge. Daddy was finally able to reach the bridge and push the little guy to the top of the bridge. I came alive and reached down and tried to grab my dad's hand, but he went down again. Finally, with the help of some of the people who had gathered, we pulled him onto the bridge. I realized then my father was only five-foot-seven, could not swim, and was in water over his head. My mother, who had been screaming frantically, came over. We all hugged Daddy and then we all started laughing. Daddy then said, "What's-a matter with you, Junior? Don't you know I can't swim?"

The funny thing is, none of us could swim. But we ended up having a very memorable day and, as you can see, one I didn't forget.

As I started writing this chapter, I was amazed how little things from the past came back so vividly. Like my brother's bathing suit with a large yellow duck on the front and my father wearing sneakers; he never wore sneakers but he did on this memorable day. Maybe if he had his big regular shoes on he might not have made it. And my excitable mother hugging and calming us all down; she never yelled at Junior, which is what I thought she would do. She just hugged him very tightly and talked softly to him. Even Madie, who all week constantly admonished Junior and me, just hugged us. This is probably why it has stuck in my mind because at that moment, that Sunday, like so many other families, I knew we, too, were a very close family.

One time, my father, who was quite a drinker, had been on the wagon for many months (so we thought). He wasn't making his trips to the Willow Bar. In fact, now he worked upstairs above the cleaners in a room by himself, just doing his tailoring work; he would never leave and my mother wondered how it seemed that he would be slightly inebriated at the end of the day. Well, I found out the answer. I happened to be patrolling on Bloomfield Avenue one morning and, as I went by the cleaners, I observed a gentleman standing under the window of the shop where Dad was working. I stopped and observed my father open the window and drop a basket on a rope to the man. I now parked my vehicle out of sight and continued to observe. The man took something out of the basket and then proceeded up Bloomfield Avenue; I watched him go into the Willow Bar. A few minutes later he came out with a bag. He then proceeded to the store, went to the basket and put the bag in it; he then tugged on the rope. I watched as my father pulled the basket up and into the window. I ran into the store and my mother and I went upstairs and confronted my father, who supposedly wasn't drinking. Of course he denied everything: "I haven't had a drink in months, Anthony."

I searched around and, under the clothes, in the large baskets I must have found at least fifteen empty bottles. In another basket, near his machine, I found a full bottle of wine. My father still claimed he wasn't drinking. He said he didn't know how the bottles got there. I immediately went to the bar and informed all the winos in the bar at the time that if any one of them brought my father any booze, I would lock them up. Of course this didn't work and it wasn't long after that my father fell down the cellar stairs, landing on his head.

Again, I was working in that area, and I was the first one to arrive when the call came in. My mother was screaming hysterically and pointing to the cellar stairs. I looked down and saw my father lying on his back on the dirt floor. I flew down the makeshift ladder; I don't think I even touched a rung. I fell to my knees and leaned down as close to him as I could. I wrapped my father in my arms; his eyes were open but he seemed to be gasping for air as I got right up in his face, holding him fast to my chest. His breath was more than warm; I will never forget that look he gave me as he very weakly said my name, "Anthony." With all the strength I could garnish, I picked him up and put him over my shoulder and, with heart pounding in every part of my body, I carried him straight up to the main floor. As I look back now, I don't know how I did it because he weighed approximately 220 pounds. But I guess the adrenaline was flowing, big time. I never gave it a thought; it was my dad and I was his first-born son. I knew I had to get him to the top as the ambulance arrived; there was no way they could have gotten a stretcher down there. We put him into the ambulance unit and rushed him to the hospital. I didn't know it then, but "Anthony" is the last word my father ever said. He suffered a cerebral hemorrhage and died a few weeks later. He's probably the reason I don't drink.

When my father didn't drink, which was rare, he was like a lamb. He would come into the cleaners in the morning and open it up around six AM. This is when he would get most of his tailoring done, before he started drinking. When I worked the midnight shift I would stop in and he would have coffee made for me; we would chat and just be close. He was always giving me good advice and building me up. I told him that I wanted to be a detective and was taking fingerprinting courses to improve my chances. Many times he said, "Anthony, don't worry, you'll make it."

I only wish he had lived to see me become a detective. Those mornings we talked and had coffee together were really special because he was sober and I realized he really was a good person; I was actually talking to the real father and not the sick one. Around that time, most people never thought about alcoholics as actually being sick. After a few conversations with him, I began to realize he was one. I did try to get him help. He would never accept any help from me, or anyone, and continued saying, "I don't have a drinking problem, son, I'm fine."

But he wasn't and, thinking about it now, I believe I should have been more forceful in getting him help because his falling accident was a direct result of his drinking.

I will always remember my father as the wise, kind man I would have coffee with while working the midnight shift. Thanks, Pop.

CHAPTER 8

REWARDING EXPERIENCES

THERE WERE MANY incidents that were not so funny. As we go further into it you will see it wasn't all laughs.

One very rewarding experience occurred when I left the beat and started working in the radio car. I was riding with Bobbie Kittrell and we were patrolling, very slowly, through the Wellmont Theater parking lot about four AM, checking the rear of the stores. I always kept my window open so I could hear outside. I thought I heard a cat cry. I asked my partner to slow down and go back through the lot. We both then heard what we thought was a cat, but, as we neared a parked auto, we stopped and got out to check the car. In the front passenger seat was what seemed like numerous blankets. Upon closer examination we observed a baby wrapped in the blankets wailing very loudly, and sounding like a cat. It wasn't a cat, it was a baby . . . obviously a newborn baby. We rushed it to the hospital and they stated that it must have been only a few hours old.

The baby survived and we checked on that baby for many weeks to make sure it was okay. I neglected to say it was

Christmas Eve when we found the baby . . . so the people at the hospital named her Mary Christmas. I checked on that baby for many years, while she was in the foundling area of the hospital; my wife and I even considered adopting her but soon she was adopted and I understand was doing very well.

Another rewarding experience for me was after a fire at an apartment building on Grove Street. It was assumed everyone had gotten out. It was a daytime fire and most of the time the people are able to get out. While the firemen were still pouring water into the front, I went to the rear and walked up the fire escape. (I was pretty good at this.) I looked in one of the windows, which was broken out. All I could see was solid smoke. I stuck my head partially in the window and thought I heard a cry for help. I climbed through the window but couldn't see much, but I was sure I heard a cry for help. I got down on the floor and looked around. I could see two legs further into the apartment. I was starting to choke from the smoke so I made my way to the sink, which was near the window I came in. I grabbed a towel that was on the sink and soaked it with water. I put it over my head and then crawled towards where I saw the legs. I finally reached an elderly gentlemen, who had become confused because of the smoke and couldn't find the door. At this point I couldn't find the door either but then I heard someone yelling to me and followed the sound of his voice. One of the patrolmen, Bill O'Connell, had seen me go in the window and was watching to make sure I came out. I'm sure glad he did, because I don't know if I would have found my way out if I didn't hear his voice. Both the gentleman and myself got out and were taken to the hospital, treated for smoke inhalation and released. Patrolman O'Connell and I both received a commendation for saving the gentleman's life.

Another time when I had to get taken to the hospital for inhalation we were sent to a house on Watching Avenue along with the County Police. It seemed a deranged man was in his house firing a shotgun out of the window and onto the street. His family had left the house and they called the police. There must have been at least thirty officers and it was about twelve noon. I ventured to the rear of the house. They had said all doors and windows were secure but I saw a cellar window slightly open. I was the only one of the policemen in the area who could fit through the window. If you saw some of the County cops there you would understand why.

I very quietly squeezed through the window, got into the cellar, snuck to the first floor and started climbing the stairs. I could see him on the second floor, leaning out a window and firing his weapon. I was about to make a move and rush him while his back was to me, and then all hell broke loose. Apparently they didn't relay to the guys in front that I had gotten into the house. They started firing tear-gas shells through first and second floor windows. I couldn't see a thing. I fell to the floor and they suddenly rushed in with their gas masks on. Thank God I was in uniform because someone grabbed me, thinking I was the perpetrator. I pointed upstairs and they went up and arrested him. I finally met him at the hospital lying on the stretcher next to me, but he was cuffed.

I have to tell you about another incident that occurred in the emergency room. Actually I was working for the hospital at the time and Bob (one of my friends) and I were doing some work at Annie's house. I was using the circular saw and don't know how but the saw slipped and cut the ends of my fingers. The blood just spouted out all over. I immediately grabbed a towel and wrapped it tightly around my hand. I was sure I lost a fingertip or two. Bob came running over. I thought I could see a slight smirk on his face but I guess he was afraid to laugh, not knowing how serious it was with the towel over my hand. He rushed me to the emergency room and I was waiting for the doctor when they brought a young girl in who was hit in the head with a bat. When I heard them talking I heard them saying she was playing softball when she got hit. When we were both left there alone for a few minutes, lying on our respective stretchers, I asked her what position she played. She told me she was an outfielder. I told her I needed an outfielder for the co-ed hospital team. Well, believe this or not, right then and there she agreed to play for us and with my good hand I was writing down her telephone number when the doctor came back in and heard us talking.

She says, "Mr. Naturale what are you doing? You ought to be ashamed of yourself."

I explained to her what I doing but she thought I was hitting on her. Hey, she was younger than my daughters. Give me a break.

Well, it turned out she was some kind of ballplayer and played with us the rest of the year. Every time I would see that doctor in the hall she would just laugh. Oh, by the way, I didn't lose any parts of my fingers.

While I'm on rewarding experiences, let me tell you about a really good one that occurred on a very quiet Saturday morning. I was assigned to the radio car uptown, which is usually quite boring. We had a report of a lost child somewhere in the area of Mills Reservation. I met the frantic mother and father of the boy near the bottom. They pointed to the top of the reservation and in the distance I could see a young boy almost to the top. I immediately called for the Fire Department and then slowly started making my way up the reservation. It just kept getting steeper and steeper and as I looked down I wondered what I was doing there so high up. I kept calling to the boy and he stopped climbing. He seemed terrified and so was I. I kept thinking the firemen would be there any moment with a very big ladder but that never happened. I kept climbing and felt like I would just tip over and fall. I hung on to tree branches and scrubs to keep from falling. I have never been so high up in my life and never knew Mills went this high.

I finally reached the young boy and he very quickly grabbed my hand. He was crying but stopped when I held him and I explained to him that everything was fine and we would be going down now. The trek down was a little easier but we were moving pretty fast and I had one hand on him and the other to grab on to anything that I could grab to slow us down. About halfway down a fireman had worked his way up and I handed the child to him. Everyone was very happy, especially the parents when we got down. After hugging their child for several minutes, both parents came over and hugged me, thanking me profusely. Believe me, I was happier than they were, not only for the child but also for myself.

What started out as a very boring day changed into quite a lot of excitement. That's the way police work was. You go from one extreme to the other and despite what some people think, we're not just giving tickets and arresting people. We also help them.

CHAPTER 9

WEIRD STORIES

WHILE A PATROLMAN, for a while I was assigned to radar. Many incidents occur when you stop people. I'm sure every police officer could relate different stories that happened to them while assigned to radar. One case I remember well while doing radar on Grove Street. I was the head car and the first officer described the car and registration to me, and I got out of the car and attempted to stop this "little red Volkswagen." Now as I stepped out towards it, the driver swerved around me, and kept going pretty fast. The driver in the car (a woman) waved to me as she sped by. I jumped into my car and gave chase. Every time I got near her she would blow the horn and speed up and raise her hand out the window.

She finally made a left on Bellevue and then another quick left into a driveway, again raising her hand in the air. I couldn't figure this out—I didn't know her. She ran into the house and as she got to the door, raised her hand again, went into the house and was gone. Her door to the car was left open so I went to it, and started to check it out. This was the middle of the day so I knew she wasn't going to run. I kept my eye on the house from her car, and in a few minutes she came running out. She came over to me and said, "Okay, Officer, give me whatever tickets you have to, I'm okay now."

I said, "You were speeding; you disregarded an officer's signal, and what's with this waving to me? I don't know you, do I?"

She said, "Officer, I'm a teacher at Grove Street School and I teach young kids, and I've instructed them whenever they have to go to the bathroom to raise their hand. Well, I'm so used to that I didn't realize I was doing it, but believe me, I had to go really bad. That's why I didn't stop."

By this time my partner had come over to assist me when I was chasing her and we both just looked at her and both agreed this must be true. No one could make up a silly story like that. She didn't get any tickets.

I was with the same partner a couple of weeks later. We were set up on South Mountain Avenue and it was early in the morning when my partner called me up to him after I had told him about a speeding car caught on my radar screen. When I got there he was standing next to the car with a woman in it. I approached them and he said, "Tony, what do you want to do here? This woman says she has a license but doesn't have it on her."

I noticed a slight smirk on his face and knew something was up. As I looked in the car I saw why she didn't have it on her. She just had a robe on—nothing else. She said to me, "Officer, as I explained to this officer, I ran out of my house in a hurry. I had just gotten out of the shower, was running late and had to take my child to school. As you can see [as she opened her robe], I didn't bring my license with me." She was right—she didn't have it or anything else but the robe on.

Now under normal circumstances we would impound the car and drive it to headquarters, but this wasn't a normal circumstance. We told her we would be leaving: "Just turn your car off and don't drive until you go home and get your license." We both left her and assumed that was what she did. Sometimes you have to use a little discretion, and this was one of those times.

Another motor vehicle violation almost crippled me. I had a car stopped on Valley by Kimberly School. I was leaning in the car window and happened to look up and see this car coming north right at me. I had to jump on the hood of the stopped vehicle to avoid getting hit. I quickly jumped in my patrol car and gave chase. They were really moving and I was blasting the siren to get them to stop. They didn't stop until they pulled into the driveway of their home in Upper Montclair with me right behind them.

It turned out to be a little old lady and she was eighty-eight years of age. She seemed quite surprised when I asked for her license. She said to me, "Why are you stopping me? Why aren't you out chasing criminals?"

I stated that she almost ran me over and was doing over sixty miles per hour in a twenty-five mile zone. She said she didn't even see the car, or me, she almost hit. Well, I gave her a summons and took her license and instructed her not to drive. I had heard she went to the Court Clerk and tried to get her license back without any success.

Sometimes a very normal circumstance turns out to be very involved. We stopped this guy in a Lincoln Continental. He was swerving all over the road. When we stopped him he couldn't produce either a license or a registration. He also smelled of liquor. We brought him into headquarters and questioned him in the back room.

He was very cooperative until we told him we would have to put him in the cellblock. When he heard this he seemed to go berserk. Now, I have to tell you he was about six-foot-five and about 250 pounds, and he was obviously a weightlifter. He had stated he was a bouncer somewhere in Paterson. He was throwing us around like dolls. We would hit him with our nightsticks and it never fazed him.

Every car was called in for assistance and we also had the

desk officers helping. We could not get him off of his feet, which is what we were trying to do. Three of us would jump on him at once and he would just knock us down. He was banging people into the walls and throwing them off of him like flyweights. Finally I got on the table and when they got him near it I jumped on him and got my arms around his neck. Everyone had been knocked off of him but I wouldn't let go. I was riding on his back and just kept squeezing his neck tighter and tighter. He would bang me up against the walls and believe me, it hurt, but I wouldn't let go and kept squeezing tighter around his neck. Finally I felt him slowing down and eventually he fell to the floor from lack of oxygen. We quickly dragged him into the cellblock and locked the door.

This guy was all muscle and it took three of us just to drag him in. He woke up in minutes and started banging on the cell bars. He did this for many hours and his arms were bleeding from hitting the bars. After about two hours he went to sleep.

The strange thing is the next day he was like a mouse. He went upstairs to the court and was arraigned and posted a bail. Another strange thing occurred. He never showed up for his court appearance and he never picked up his car, which was impounded, and he never showed up at his place of employment. When we checked the car serials, all had been filed down and the car was untraceable. It's like the guy disappeared from the face of the earth. I think he disappeared all right, but not from the face of the earth.

As a patrolman, when we worked days we would sometimes be assigned to the motorcycle squad. I had never ridden a motorcycle before so for me this was a lot of fun. The steady guys would train the younger guys so we could ride them while they were off. First we trained on the three-wheelers. They were easy, but all you would do is give parking tickets. This wasn't too exciting. Now the two-wheelers were something else. I couldn't believe the power they had.

One time I was working uptown and I was showing off a

little bit to my wife, who was wheeling my son Steven in the carriage on Grove Street. Now as I zipped by, she said later, I looked so good with my sunglasses on and sitting high on the seat. Actually I slowly went by them a couple of times.

After I passed them I approached Watchung Avenue, and a small truck went through the red traffic light at Watchung Avenue, and turned right onto Grove Street. I thought, oh boy, my first moving violation on the motorcycle. I started to follow him and was going to stop him, but he speeded it up. He was unaware I was behind him. I thought I'd follow him a little further until I stopped him, and get him for speeding also. Well, there were a couple of problems. First of all, it had rained a lot the night before and some of the streets were a little wet. Secondly, he didn't know I was going to pass him in an attempt to stop him. Now I guess I should have stayed behind him and blasted the siren until he stopped, but being new at this I was still having problems finding everything. I pushed what I thought was the siren and it was the horn.

Now the third thing, and probably the most damaging to me, was as I was attempting to pass him, he started to make a left-hand turn into Tuxedo Road. He was slowing down and I thought it was because he saw me, but he was slowing to make the turn. Now I'm sure you can picture this because I sure can, many years later. As he was turning I kept turning with him to avoid getting hit head-on. Somewhere during his turn, he finally spotted me—he could have touched me, he was so close. He was more surprised than me but thank God he had good reflexes because he stopped in the middle of his turn, and of course I kept going. I was going too fast to stop, so I kept going over the curb, up in the air and down on the ground. Of course I didn't go down with the motorcycle, I went through the air by myself. The motorcycle didn't go down either, it kept going and was finally stopped at the church steps. I didn't go that far. When it hit the curb I went straight up in the air about ten feet and landed with a resounding thud. My head hit first and the rest of my body followed. I hit so hard that the peak of my hat jammed into my nose, cutting it, forcing the hat down over my head (we didn't wear helmets then). My arms and feet, especially my elbows, sunk into the mud about four or five inches. My hat was jammed onto my head so hard I had difficulty getting it off. Thank God I did before any people arrived because they were starting to. What really saved me from getting hurt, other than some minor lumps and bruises, was the soft mud. With the help from the violator I was able to get the motorcycle up and actually got it running. After his help I couldn't even give him a ticket.

The really funny part of this is the beat-up me, and the beat-up motorcycle, limped back towards my house on Grove Street. We were just chugging along and there's my wife and son. She said, "Anthony, what happened?" Would you believe it? She started laughing. But this happens all the time with her. Whenever I get hurt or fall, she breaks out into laughter. She's laughed an awful lot during our forty-seven years of marriage. (It must be nervous laughter.) Well, eventually I cleaned up and went in to report the incident.

I had one more motorcycle incident that sticks out in my mind, shortly after the Grove Street incident. I was riding on Brunswick Road and was getting near Valley Road when a dog started chasing me. He kept going for my right leg and I kept lifting it up so I wouldn't get bitten. Now, I guess I was paying too much attention to him and not enough to the cycle, because all of a sudden I was at Valley Road and still moving pretty fast, trying to get away from the dog. I had to do something or I would go straight across Valley Road and into the house right across from Brunswick Road.

I got into the intersection and turned right, very sharply, right onto Valley Road. I was going too fast to make the turn and I fell over right into the intersection. As the cycle hit the ground I jumped and fell to the ground so the cycle didn't land on me. It didn't but a car coming north was right on top of me. I can remember this like it was yesterday. You don't forget moments like that. I really thought this was it, but the woman driver swerved and went around me, narrowly missing me. I don't know how she did it but I'm sure glad she did or I wouldn't be here right now. Whoever said women weren't good drivers? I certainly didn't agree with that. The woman stopped to assist me and I immediately took a liking to her. She said she was on her way to church. I'm so glad it was Sunday and she went to church.

I never really liked riding anything with just two wheels anyway. That was basically the end of my motorcycle career.

A lot of things occur when you're off-duty. One such incident occurred when we were at Tierney's Tavern. I was with Skippy Rizzie (the same one) and Willie Walsh, who later became the Chief of Detectives at the Prosecutor's Office. We all had a couple of beers and came out onto Valley Road, when believe it or not we observed a coke sale just a few feet in front of the Tavern. We approached them and told them we were the police. The one guy said, "You guys aren't cops— you just came out of the Tavern."

I said, "So what? Cops don't drink?"

"Let me see your badge," he said.

I said, "Skip, show him your badge." Skip said he didn't have it. "Okay, Willie, show him your badge." He said he didn't have his either.

The suspect laughed and said to me, "How about you, you got a badge?"

"No, sir, I don't, but I do have this gun," and held it to his head, "and this says we are cops and you, sir, are under arrest."

He said he believed me and immediately complied. He was quite a catch. He had a record a mile long for drug sales. We put him away for quite some time. After that incident we all made sure we had our badges with us at all times.

Another time, with Skippy again, we were able to apprehend a criminal who had just escaped from police headquarters. We were just leaving from a PBA meeting and as we were traveling in my car past the police station, we saw a guy running out the front door of the police station towards Bloomfield Avenue. About ten feet behind him we saw the Desk Sergeant and a patrolman chasing him. This guy was young and fast and was opening the gap between them. Now fortunately for us, the light was green and the road was clear so I kept driving the same way he was running. We crossed Valley Road and I figured if we got far enough ahead, we could stop the car in front of him and grab him. Well, my figuring was pretty good because once I was past him I made a quick left turn into the parking lot so we could jump out and grab him. The timing was so good we didn't even have to grab him. He ran right into the side of my vehicle at full speed, fell to the ground and was out like a light. We just stood over him and in less than a minute the two policemen arrived very slowly and out of breath. They very sheepishly took their prisoner and brought him back to Headquarters. They did thank us.

Whenever I looked at the dent he put in the side of my car I thought of that perpetrator—and no, I didn't report this accident to the insurance company.

It wasn't just criminals that were the danger in police work. Sometimes the elements can be dangerous too. I was working in the radio car uptown one very rainy night. The winds were excessive and many power lines were coming down. I came across one on Watchung Avenue between Fullerton and The Plaza. This line was right in the middle of the street and was actually melting the tar. I got in front of it and used my flashing red light to keep anyone from going over it.

Now, this line was bouncing on the street and arcing as it kept hitting the street. Public Service had been notified and I was instructed to stand by until they arrived. I wasn't content to sit in the car and wait. I got out in the teeming rain with my raincoat and boots on and got nearer to the line. Being an electrician, I believed I knew something about these power lines. I traced it back to the stores and it seemed to be the secondary line coming from the transformer. Believing this could only be 240 volts, I went to the spot where it was arcing in the street. I grabbed the line from the end on the wet insulation and pulled it from the center of the street. As I pulled it to the side, it kept bouncing back into the street to where it originally was. So I grabbed it and bent it around the meter near the curb so it wouldn't be in the middle of the street.

Soon after the Public Service man arrived, he questioned me about how it got bent around the meter. I explained to him what I had done and he flatly said, "No, you didn't." We argued back and forth a few minutes, then he said, "Look, pal, if you did that you would have been burned to the street."

I said, "How do you think the line got wrapped round the meter? Besides, it's only 240 volts. I checked it coming from the transformer."

He said, "You better look again, pal. It's 24,000 volts on the primary side of the transformer."

We both then followed the line and would you believe it—he was right. It was the primary side. He then said the only explanation is the breaker kicked. He called it in and they said no, the breaker was still on. Besides, it was still arcing. He looked at me very strangely and said, "Mister, I don't know how you're still alive."

We never found an explanation for this. My explanation was, "It wasn't my time yet." After that, I left all power lines to the Public Service men.

CHAPTER 10

THE DETECTIVE BUREAU

WHEN I BECAME a detective, I was assigned to the Identification Bureau. I took a course on my own to get myself qualified as an "expert." This course was a lot of fun because I used to practice taking prints with my kids. I would explain to them how it worked. It was great, because if one of the kids went into an area in the house they weren't supposed to be in (for example, where my weapons were locked up), I would ask them who did it. No one would say a thing. Then I would take out my fingerprint kit and say, "Well, I'll just have to check for prints." I never had to—one of them would always come forward and admit it. I would also tell them I could tell if they were lying by checking their pulse. This usually worked until they got a little older. I even tried it on my wife. It didn't work with her.

I can remember one of my kids constantly coming up to me if we questioned something they did. They would say, "Check my pulse, Dad, and you'll see I didn't do it." I also fingerprinted many of our neighbors, but I believe they complied very reluctantly.

While I was studying this course as a patrolman, the Detective Bureau actually used me on jobs to pick up prints when their man wasn't available. This helped establish me as a fingerprint expert and when the job became available, they had to give it to me. There was no other patrolman who was qualified.

When I first got into the ID Bureau, I heard they hadn't picked up prints to capture anyone for twelve years. When I was there about six months I was able to do it at least three times. The first time is unforgettable.

On one Sunday I was working, and after much eye-straining and searching I made a match. What a great feeling that was. The guy I got (one of the Smiths) had committed about fourteen burglaries. I got a partial print off the glass from the window he had broken to get into the building.

The Captain who headed that bureau was very knowledgeable and helpful. He stated I was the first qualified print man they gave him in a long time. Captain Karas, my supervisor, had been in the Identification Bureau for most of his time on the job. He joined after having been discharged from the US Army after a very illustrious stint in the Seventh Army as one of General George Patton's scouts serving in France. He was the recipient of the Purple Heart and the Bronze Star.

His luck changed somewhat, however, after joining the Police Department. After only two months on the job as a probationary patrolman, he was sent to New Street on a family disturbance. Before he got into the house the irate boyfriend fired a shotgun at him, hitting him in the leg while he was at the corner of New Street and Bloomfield Avenue. After numerous operations he had to have a portion of his leg removed. Because he was a probationary patrolman, the town wanted to release him but later decided not to. He was assigned to the Identification Bureau and worked his way up to Captain and in charge of the Bureau. It was a good decision for the town because the Captain became quite a well-known fingerprint expert and was used as an expert in many court cases. He also taught me fingerprinting and photography as well as all other Identification duties. Thanks, Captain.

One of my first photography jobs in the Identification Bureau was very memorable. Not only do I remember it from at the scene, but when I was going to Montclair State College I had to write a paper on "Love" and really got into this one crime that I thought was an act of love. In fact my professor, after reading it, wanted to publish it and (you'll never believe this) when I brought it up to his class the next day, I learned our class was canceled. It seemed our professor had a heart attack and had died. Wow, what luck—but his luck was much worse than mine. He was only in his forties. The article never got published.

Well, here's the very short story titled "An Act of Love."

A prominent physician who lived in Montclair seemed to have everything: money, a large home with a pool, servants, a very loving wife and young son.

The only problem, which wasn't a problem while he was young, was that his son was retarded and they knew his condition could not improve. They loved him so much and would not consider institutionalizing him, so they took the burden on and cared for him themselves. This doctor and his wife were so devoted to their son they did everything with him and for him. One of them was always with him and loving and caring for him.

As the couple aged, the boy had grown to be well over 200 pounds and was becoming too much for them to handle. Although they always had physical help, the boy would only respond to one of them.

Now the mother, in her sixties, contracted a deadly cancer. The father had given up his lucrative physician practice to care for both his wife and son full time. The burden, however, was becoming too great for him. He could hardly lift either one of them and his health was also beginning to fail him. He loved them both so much, he couldn't bear to put them both in homes. Not only that, they would all be separated, and that had never happened before.

Out of his love for them, he did what he believed was the only answer. He went to his bedroom and got a .38 fully loaded revolver and went to his wife's room. She was almost incoherent now but we believe she heard his last words, which were "I love you," prior to fatally shooting her.

He then repeated this in his son's room. Before he turned the weapon on himself he wrote a short note saying, "I love my wife and son so much and can no longer take care of them. Please forgive me."

This was classified as a double murder and suicide. At this time I was a detective in the Identification Bureau taking pictures, and this was one of my first assignments and a very memorable one.

While I was in that department I would also take pictures of accidents and develop all the department's pictures. This was so interesting that for a time, I thought I would be a photographer. That didn't last long.

One thing that sticks in my mind is a young boy in his early teens who used to ride on his bicycle and chase police cars, being at a lot of the accident scenes. I would take pictures and he would follow me and ask me questions. He was so interested in the photos that I would let him come into the Identification Bureau and show him how I developed film. He was very interested and seemed to learn pretty fast. Then I didn't see him for a while.

Many years later I saw him as a young reporter in New York City. I watched him progress up the ranks and just recently I saw him working with the "20-20" TV series. I followed his career through newspaper and TV reports, and he became quite famous as a crime reporter for the New York Police Department. Many times I wanted to contact him. Maybe I will through this book if it ever gets completed.

One thing I wanted him to know is, "John, the warrants you got in Montclair kept getting pushed to the bottom of the pile." When John was doing crime reporting, he was obviously called all hours during the night so he left his car on the street, and in Montclair you get tickets if you leave your car on the street between two AM and five AM. As a result, the warrants totaled up for him. The funny thing about this is my boss (I was also in charge of the warrant squad at the time) wanted me to go to Channel Five, while John was reporting, and serve the warrants to him personally. I don't know if he was kidding or not but I refused to do it. John Miller is presently a co-host with Barbara Walters on the television program "20/20."

In the Identification Bureau we also were in charge of all gun permits that were issued. We had to investigate the applicants and if they checked out okay, we would issue the permit.

We had a young mother come in, and as usual, our question was, "Why do you want to own a gun?"

This woman we'll call Betty smiled and said, "I want to kill my husband." The Captain and I both stopped in our tracks. She then started laughing and said, "Hey, I'm only kidding." We did send her prints in and they came back "no record." We delayed her permit but eventually we had to give her the permit.

Needless to say, the following Christmas, Betty killed her husband. Now there were numerous circumstances to this. He was constantly beating her and her kids. She never called the police so we didn't have a record of it. He did have an extensive drug record and the day of the shooting he broke down the door, which she had locked, and came at her. She shot him as he broke though the door. She was charged with murder. We felt quite relieved after her sentencing. The murder charges were reduced to "justifiable homicide."

While I was working in the Detective Bureau I would sometimes be assigned to the Investigative Bureau with another detective. One night we had to go to Totowa and pick up a young girl on a warrant for "bad checks." We brought her to the ID Bureau for processing. While we were there, the other detective, Paul, had to run out on an emergency. Normally one person wouldn't be left alone with a woman, but we figured he would be right back and the desk was just below us.

This is going to be hard to believe but it's true. What is hard to believe are the circumstances.

First of all, there was a door leading to outside the police department right where she was sitting. You could open that door, walk down the stairs and be outside on Bloomfield Avenue. Secondly, I didn't have my handcuffs with me. The final problem was the detective stayed much longer than we had anticipated. I was typing her arrest report, fingerprinting her and taking her photo, and this all took over one half-hour.

Now the last and most important circumstance was that I really had to relieve myself. As I sat there typing I was getting more and more uncomfortable. I couldn't call for help from the desk downstairs because they were all out on emergencies. And could you imagine me calling the desk downstairs and saying, "Sergeant, would you send someone up here because I have to take a leak." No, I wouldn't do that. Plus I kept thinking my partner would be back any minute.

The girl saw that I was squirming in my seat and said, "What's-a matter, Officer?"

I said, "If you must know, I have to go to the bathroom."

She said, "Go ahead, I won't look."

Now the bathroom was a little behind me but around a corner, so I wouldn't be able to actually see her. A bright idea came to me. "Give me all your jewelry," I said, which she did. I got a few feet away, headed towards the bathroom and thought, this is probably all stolen and she's just going to unlock that door and walk away. How would I explain that? Then I heard her move, and I jumped out from the doorway of the bathroom. "Okay, here's your stuff back."

"What's the matter, Officer, don't you have to go anymore?"

"Yes, I do," I said, "but I can't take the chance on you walking out."

She swore she wouldn't but I didn't know her from Adam and couldn't take the chance. I started typing again and boy, now I really had to go. I was almost ready to go in my pants when another idea came to me. "Look," I said, "I want you to hum."

"Hum?" she said. "What do you want me to hum?"

"Just hum anything, but do it quick."

"Okay, but I don't have a very good voice."

So she stated humming and she was right—she didn't have a good voice. I slowly backed towards the bathroom. Suddenly she stopped and I ran out towards her. "What happened? Why did you stop?"

She said, "Oh, I was just testing you, Officer."

Now I was really about ready to go in my pants at this time so I said, "Look, hurry up and hum and keep on humming."

So she started again and this time I got to the bathroom. I have to let you know I had to go in spurts so I could still hear her. Well, needless to say everything came out all right and she got bailed out—and yes, I did wash my hands.

Now the irony of this is the very next day I'm typing in

the ID Bureau, and the same door I was worried about was open. This hallway leads to the courtroom as well as outside. Would you believe it? Here comes the "Hummer." She comes walking by the door (no, she wasn't humming) with her lawyer and sees me from the hallway and stops and sticks her head in the door and yells out very loudly, "Hi, Officer—I'm still humming."

Well, my Captain, who's sitting right next to me, asks, "What's she mean by that?"

I said, "Captain, you wouldn't believe it if I told you."

A few months down the line he retired and we took him out for lunch, and I told him the whole story. He said, "Tony, you ought to write a book."

There is just a little something that I would like to add to this story. It actually just happened a few days ago, but I felt I should add it. I was talking to my young ten-year-old granddaughter, Emily, and her friend Megin, also around ten. They were asking me questions about the book I was writing and wanted to have me tell them a story that was in it. So "The Hummer" is the first one that came to mind and I related the whole incident. Now Megin said, "You arrested her for humming?" No, I said. Then I had to explain why she was arrested. My granddaughter then told Megin that her Pop-Pop couldn't come out of the bathroom because "his pants was down." Megin said, "Oh, I see."

I just left it at that but thought it would be a good ending to the hummer story.

Det. Rocco, Phil Wagner, me and Robert Thompson.
Paraphenilia seized after arresting burglars that had
committed numerous burglaries.

Members of the Detective Bureau show Public Safety Commissioner Richard Pettingill the narcotics they confiscated in a raid Friday night. From left are Detectives Herman Hartsfield, Richard Tait, Anthony Naturale, John McGill, Commissioner Pettingill, Thomas Sobers and Robert Cummings.

◄ Graduation from
Montclair State
University 1975.

Getting congratulations
from Sen. Richard
Codey, sponsor of the
L.E.A.P. program.

MAY 29, 1975

THE GRADUATES - Assemblyman Richard Codey (D-
26), center, offers congratulations to Patrolman Robert
F. McKaig of the Montclair Police Department on the
completion of his studies at Montclair State College. Ptl.
McKaig and three fellow members of the department,
from left, Sgt. Anthony Naturale, Lt. John P. Corcoran,
and Ptl. Anthony C. Acocella, will graduate on Sunday.

All the police department men participated in student
teaching programs. They studied under the LEEP
program (Law Enforcement Educational Program).

Assemblyman Codey recently introduced a bill which
would permit the state to assist municipalities in
granting policemen incentive pay for college credit.

CAPTAINS MEET JIM—
Captains of the Montclair
Fire and Police Departments
take a few moments to meet
with Channel 2 newscaster
Jim Jensen, who guided his
CBS All-Stars in a benefit
softball game for NEDAC last
Tuesday at Montclair State.
From left, are Fireman Stevie
Miscia, Police Detective
Sergeant Thomas Oates and
Police Detective Lieutenant
Anthony Naturale.

➤ 'THE NATURALE'—Tony
Naturale shows form almost
equal to that of Robert
Redford in the movie "The
Natural" as he tosses a pitch
in the benefit game between
the Montclair Police
Department and the New
Jersey Devils.

Lt. Naturale as Head of Internal Affairs, 1985

CHAPTER 11

1969—BUZZ ALDRIN

DURING THE PERIOD of time while working in the Identification Bureau we had many historic events take place. This was 1969, a very memorable year. Heck, you could buy a loaf of bread for 23 cents and a gallon of gas for 35 cents. Of course the minimum wage was only $1.60 an hour. And it

was also the year of the miraculous New York Mets and the
Australian Rod Laver who won the Tennis Grand Slam. But
these were only historic events to sports fans. We had the
Newark Riots, which affected many people. Then we had
the Woodstock Festival in New York, which changed the
direction of many people's lives.

In 1968 Donald Stake and I had bought a small rooming
house on Broad Street in Newark. I don't know why, because
we certainly didn't make much money on it. We would go
down there each week and he would sit in the car while I
would go up there and try and collect rents. It didn't hurt
that I was armed and I let them see my weapon. I only had
to pull it out once, when one of the tenants came at me with
a knife. He was all drugged up but immediately stopped when
I pulled the gun out. He very sheepishly handed me the ten
dollars he owed me. I felt like I was holding him up but I did
put my gun away before I accepted the money. Hey, we owned
the house, remember? (But not for long.)

A few weeks after that incident the Newark Riots started
(we had nothing to do with it, honest) and we never went
back to Newark again to collect rents. Our venture went
bankrupt and the building was demolished, like many
buildings in Newark. And of course we know that changed
the direction of many more people's lives.

Also during 1969 we had the first man land on the moon,
Neil Armstrong, and as most everyone knows, Buzz Aldrin,
the second man to set foot on the moon, was a Montclair
native. He was a 1948 Montclair High School graduate.

Now Montclair was having quite a big homecoming for
him, and of course the Police Department had to assist with
protection during the motorcade and then afterwards at
Montclair State College, where they were having a dinner for
him. All the detectives (including me) were issued small
security pins, which the Treasury Department handed out.
We had to wear them on our jacket lapels so other officers
would know all the plainclothes men. All of the detectives

walked alongside of the car carrying Buzz Aldrin up
Bloomfield Avenue through town and by his former residence
on Princeton Place.

That evening we were assigned to Montclair State College
for the dinner. We were all assigned to different tables. This
was quite an honor and I was even able to talk to Buzz for a
short period of time. I didn't sit at his table but I was at the
table with his sister and other relatives. In talking to his sister,
she remarked about how she liked the pins that we had on
our lapels. She told me one of the treasury agents gave her
one pin, and she needed another one, because she wanted
to make earrings out of them. She then asked me what I was
going to do with mine. I said, "I'm going to give it to you
because I don't wear earrings," and I still don't. She was very
pleased.

However, my wife wasn't because she said she *did* wear
earrings and would have loved to have a pair of earrings made
from this historic event.

Sorry, dear. Next time Buzz goes to the moon I'll give you
my pin.

CHAPTER 12

THE BURGLAR ALARM BUSINESS

AFTER I LEFT the ID Bureau, I made Sergeant and as I stated earlier, I was able to spend more time on the street. I saw that many people who were burglarized needed burglar alarms, so being an electrician, I had some knowledge of this. I took a course on alarms and used a couple of detectives to assist me, and we started putting in alarms on our off time. We became very busy so I hired my good friend Frank Zaremba, who was an electronics expert. He was really good. He would make up the alarm boxes and we would wire the job.

Frank was really a great friend. He and his wife, Dolores, would go out with my wife and me. We were very compatible. At work we would laugh the whole time. Things would happen to me and Frank would say, "I don't believe it." Frank named this book—he said it so many times. After a while he began to say, "I believe it—I believe it."

The funny thing is when he started working for me, I was paying him $6.00 an hour. After one week he said, "Tony, you know I'm worth more."

Without hesitation I said, "Okay, Frank, how about $12.00 an hour?" He agreed.

A few weeks later he said, "Tony, I'm worth more."

I said, "Okay, Frank. How about us being partners?"

So we were for a very short period of time and then Frank came up to me and said, "Tony, I don't think there's enough work here for partners."

I said, "What do you want, Frank?"

He said, "Tony, can I fire you and I keep the business?"

I said, "Okay, Frank, you own the business. You may even keep the truck and the tools."

"Great," he said. So I started working for Frank.

Frank was pretty shrewd, huh? Well, to tell you the truth, it was becoming too much for me. I had a full-time job and Frank didn't. He did most of the work anyway, while I was on my regular job, and besides, he was my friend. What are friends for?

Frank did quite well with the alarm business and every once in a while he would hire me, especially with the electrical end of it. (He didn't pay me as well as I paid him.) He and I worked so much on alarms in the Montclair area that when we would go into people's houses, they knew I was a Lieutenant with the Police Department and everyone thought he was too.

Everyone liked Frank. We all miss him very much.

While we were doing these jobs, it seemed there were more and more burglaries. A certain Lieutenant on the Police Department who was working steady midnights, which he requested, would call me in the AM and tell me where all the hits were. I would tell Frank and he would go see them to see if they wanted an alarm installed. Every job we got, Frank would give this Lieutenant $25.00 for the lead. After a while, we started to get suspicious. Frank and I decided we wouldn't tell him about any of the jobs we did and certainly not take any more leads from him.

Now, the bar and liquor store around the corner from the police station had a window security but no alarm in the store, é

and the store owner was suspicious of one of his workers (it wasn't the Lieutenant). So Frank and I went in there during the night (before the midnight shift) and installed "electric eyes" with a beam crossing where the cash register was. Would you believe it, that night this Lieutenant, who was working the desk, walked around the corner and very calmly removed a front glass (that wasn't taped), went in and opened the cash register, crossing the beam, setting off the alarm. Of course he heard it on his radio and very quickly backed out the same window. As he was doing this, a radio car pulled up and the Lieutenant ordered the patrolmen to go check the rear of the store, which they had to do. The patrolmen, Roger Spain and Jim Berry, went to the rear and very wisely made a call to the Captain in charge of the Detective Bureau.

At this point in time most of us were suspicious of the Lieutenant but couldn't catch him in the act. The Captain and Deputy Chief came in and were going to confront the Lieutenant, but would you believe it, he went back to the police desk, put his raincoat on and started out across the street to hit another store. In the middle of the intersection of Bloomfield and Midland Avenues, they all converged on him with their weapons drawn. He raised his hands in the air and a bolt-cutter fell to the ground. We found out later he thought he had gotten away with the first job, and was heading across the street to break into another store. He went for about fifteen jobs but we all knew he had done many more. He even had, in his car trunk, coffee cans filled with quarters taken from the parking meters. Firemen used to see him emptying the meters, but they assumed that was his assignment. It seemed when he broke into the court clerk's office (which he admitted) he stole the meter keys. I even believe he broke into my house while we were at a wake. He was seen in front of my house at the time we believe it was broken into. Well, we couldn't prove it but everything seems to point in that direction, and he was never charged for it.

We got many calls after his arrest came out implicating him in other jobs. One woman even said she talked to the

Lieutenant because she was afraid to keep her money in the store. He convinced her to hide it in one of the ceiling blocks, which she did. The next day the money was gone.

This guy could have written a book. He went to jail, and after about four years got out, got a job with a real estate agency and was selling houses. After a few months he was caught again, this time breaking into houses. The last I heard he was still in jail.

Another job Frank helped me with was the little confectionery store around the corner from Headquarters. The woman complained that people were stealing her magazines and stuff and the only ones it could be were the police. She came in about six AM and the only ones who were there when she came in were policemen.

So Frank and I proceeded to observe it. She was right: mostly only police did come in with the exception of a few other town workers. We snuck in late at night—Frank drove and I hid down in the seat so no policeman would see me. We went through the back and set up two peephole cameras with a VCR to record our findings. We also put a sticker on the front door to legalize the taping (a very small sticker). After the shift we retrieved the tapes. Frank went over all the tapes while I went to work. Anything suspicious he would pull out, and I would check them.

We sure found some irregularities. A couple of officers actually went behind the counter and took all kinds of food from the refrigerators. Some took magazines, some cigarettes and miscellaneous items. We ran it for another day and got the same thing. All the while this was occurring, the guy who worked for the owner just sat at one of the stools and did nothing. He had obviously seen all this. Some of the officers did pay and actually rang up their own items.

I made contact with the State Police Undercover Unit. They investigated Police Departments. Two investigators looked at the tapes with me. They agreed we had something and would get back to me. They wanted to install more tapes along with the sound.

A couple of days later the Chief contacted me and stated the State would not get involved. They wanted us to first take it to the Prosecutor's Office. It seems the higher up you go, the more politics enters.

The detectives and I had it covered pretty well, but it seems they didn't want to step on another agency's toes. Hey, I knew that would happen; that's why I didn't go that way in the first place. So you know what happened? The first thing they did was call in the County. They didn't investigate like the State was going to do. They just looked at my tapes, and sent a notice to the man who worked there who was allowing this to happen. They sent him a written notice that they wanted to speak to him about the thefts. What does he do? The next night we observed on the camera him showing the officers the letter he got from the County and probably asking them what he should do. I don't know what they told him to do, but the night before he was to appear he attempted to commit suicide by cutting both wrists. He ended up in the hospital. We kept a tape in the store and the next night when I checked them, one of the policemen was holding up money in the air. He didn't know where the cameras were but he certainly knew there were cameras there. So much for that investigation.

The Chief told me he would hold the tapes and see if we could file departmental charges on the officers. That never happened.

The owner of the store was so upset she notified the *Herald News*. They had quite an article in the paper, but that was the end of it. When I retired the tapes were still in the Chief's safe.

Ironically, while writing this chapter, Grange Habermann, my friend the writer (who's helping me) and I stopped in to Cohen's to try and get more facts. We walked in and there was Estelle and her son, Scott, near the front door. She immediately stated, "Lieutenant Naturale, I can't believe it— this is our last day here and you show up. We are having a party for our last day for all of our friends and I want you to stay." I did politely decline but she gave me a three-page letter outlining the events from the beginning of my investigation and until the Prosecutor's Office took over. This was the first time I had seen this letter and I felt it best not to include it in the story because none of the policemen had been charged, but I did appreciate her kind words.

One alarm job we did turned out to be pretty funny (I think). It was at a local cemetery in the south end of town. Actually the Lieutenant we arrested gave us the lead. Coincidentally, he actually worked at the cemetery part-time. They were getting thefts from their office (I wonder who could have done it). So we proceeded to wire the exterior and set up electric eyes inside.

Now, I did all the climbing. (I was pretty good at this.) I was at the top of the furnaces and somehow I slipped and fell to the ground (I was good at this also), knocking numerous small boxes over at the foot of the furnaces. These boxes all had ashes in them and had names on the boxes. Unfortunately the ashes all spilled out of the individual boxes. We didn't know what to do so we scooped up all the ashes and put a little in each box. We tried to spread them evenly; however, we didn't know who the big people (lots of ashes) and the little people (small amount) were. We hoped that they didn't weigh them, and there were no DNA tests then, so we felt safe. I'm sure they all are now resting in peace.

We worked there until very late at night. It was about one AM and I had finished my end of the job, so I started looking around. It was very dark and I discovered a Victrola (an old music machine) and it had a record on it. I started it up and it very loudly started playing "Rock Of Ages . . ." It had been so quiet and when this came on it reverberated throughout the building. In seconds Frank came running over to me yelling, "Tony, what's that?" You had to be there— I started laughing and poor Frank was ashen. He finally started laughing too but we relived that scene many times.

CHAPTER 13

HELP FROM THE FBI

AS A SERGEANT on the street, I had much more free time to observe things. I noticed a lot of activity around this little confectionery store. In fact a few of the policemen, mostly higher-ranking officers, went in there quite often (both on and off-duty) and were not bringing out any packages. This alone wasn't odd, but the fact that when I approached them in the store to talk with them, they would very quickly leave or ignore me. The owner, who I used to talk to a lot, acted very nervous while I was in there with them. Now this got my interest. I made contact with a young boy in the neighborhood who would give me info now and then and tell me about the neighborhood thieves. He said, "Man, don't you know that's a bookie joint and those guys cover for him? But I would be careful because he's run by the Big Guys." Well, I knew it now and I certainly couldn't ignore it.

For about one month I kept a log on what I saw and sure enough, the kid seemed to be right. I approached my immediate Lieutenant and informed him of my findings. I was sure he was honest and not tied in. Well, this is what he said: "Tony, I think you're right but I don't want to get involved." He was on the Captain's list and I guess he didn't want to upset the apple cart.

So I went to my Captain, who I was sure was honest, and this is what he said: "Tony, just watch your back." He seemed to be aware of what was happening, but said he couldn't help me.

Well, one of the officers going in the store was higher up than the Captain, so now what do I do? I wasn't going to let this go, so I did what they say you're not supposed to do—go to another agency. I contacted the Federal Bureau of Investigation and few days later, a couple of agents met me at my mother's sheltered care home. I told everyone there, who knew me quite well, that they were insurance agents (even my mother). Well, they *were* agents.

I informed the agents of my findings, and within a few days they had surveillance set up in an apartment across the street. No one within the department but me was involved. One of the undercover agents got so close to the owner, and trusted him so much, he offered him a piece of the action.

After a few days they contacted me and showed me pictures of the people going in and out. I had to identify the ones who were the police officers, which I did. I was then instructed by the agents to hit the place looking for numbers, which we knew he had. Well, we hit the place, as one of my normal "gambling functions" (I was at that time head of the one-man gambling squad) and with other detectives (agents were there on the scene when we got there), we found numerous numbers slips hidden in the oven.

Now, they didn't even take the suspect to our Headquarters. They took him directly to the Newark FBI office and interrogated him there, in an attempt to get the names of any officers involved. This man was really frightened. They questioned him for hours and he wouldn't give up anyone else. He stated this operation was strictly on his own and no one else was involved. There were never any police or anyone else charged. He took the full brunt of it and spent about four years in jail. To this day, no one is sure who brought the Feds in, until now I guess (if they read this book).

Well, I was the top choice at the time because I was making numerous gambling arrests, and raiding most of the gambling clubs around town. The only good that came out of it was there were no more numbers at that spot, and the police who were involved were a little leery of allowing this to happen. Ironically, they couldn't say anything, because if they did it would appear that they were involved.

Another irony of this particular story is that I was friendly with the owner and after he got out of prison (about four years later), I met him at a party of a friend of mine. It seems my friend was related to him, and we were both invited. I saw him there eyeing me. He looked nice and healthy and tan. He finally came over to me, and started talking. "Tony," he said, "I know it was you."

I said, "What are you talking about?"

This went on for a short time, then he said, "Look, I know you were just doing your job."

I said, "Mister, I know what happened because I made the numbers arrest, but that's all I know about it. I don't know why they took you to Newark."

He said, "Well, I know you do and I just want you to know I couldn't give anybody up or I would be dead right now. I put my time in and now I'm clean. I don't mess with numbers anymore and I have no animosity towards you." He shook my hand and we parted as friends.

While I was doing gambling surveillances, I had access to the County, both their men and equipment. One vehicle was a "hippie van" with a window on top and a periscope that you could look through. I would gather information through surveillance at different bookie joints, then bring it to the County and draw up the search warrants. Sometimes, while you're watching that, another crime occurs. Naturally, you have to take some action. This one incident really sticks in my mind, because I almost had a heart attack.

While watching a store on Bloomfield Avenue, a silent alarm sounded at Headquarters. You won't believe this, but Frank and I installed this alarm at Caruso's Garage. I ran from my vehicle to the back of the building just as the perpetrator was exiting the rear window. He ran north on the tracks. I was about fifteen feet behind him and could see he was young and fast. Now, fortunately for me, I was doing a lot of jogging and was in pretty good shape. I knew I had to pace myself because there were no other officers in sight. I just tried to keep pace with him.

After what seemed like about two miles of running (but was only about a quarter of a mile), I saw that he was slowing down. I then gave it all I had and narrowed the distance. When he turned around to see where I was, he was so surprised he slowed even more. That's when I made a big lunge and was able to grab his shirt and pull him in. I was so tired I had to sit on him for a few minutes to catch my breath until other officers arrived.

I was in plainclothes and he didn't believe I was a cop. He said, "No cop can catch me." He finally believed me after he was arrested. I remember telling him he smoked too much. I'm glad he did because if he didn't, I probably never would have caught him.

While I was working with the police, I was working part-time with a local electrician and was able to utilize their electrical truck. I was actually doing a job for the company and was working in the hallway of a two-family house. The second-floor apartment had the door open and I could see into the apartment. While I was there numerous men came up and down the stairs. I recognized most of them as local drug users. It appeared the woman in the apartment was actually selling them drugs. I went back to my truck and got my police radio. I explained the situation to the Narcotic

Detectives. I went back upstairs and started working on the fixture again. Now each time a person appeared to make a buy I forwarded the info by whispering into my radio. We did this for over an hour and the Narcotics Detectives, who had stationed themselves near the house after I called, arrested about twenty people who made buys. They waited until the subjects had pulled away from the house so the next buyer wouldn't see them.

A little later I had to go back to Headquarters to fill out my report and there was the woman who was selling the drugs. She was being booked at the desk. She immediately recognized me and said, "Hey, electrician, did they arrest you too?" I said, "They have electrical problems too." I then walked over to the Desk Sergeant and asked him where the electrical short was. He got the drift and pointed to the back room. I have seen that woman on the streets numerous times and she still believes that I'm an electrician.

Another time while I was working with the electrician I stopped in Ray's Luncheonette for coffee. There were only two of us at the counter, and then a man walked in and went to the end of the counter and spoke to the owner. He whispered so I couldn't hear them, but the owner gave me a quick glance and seemed very nervous. The man then quickly left. I jumped up and followed him out. I got his plate number as he quickly pulled off.

I went back in and questioned the owner about him. He was very reluctant to talk but finally said, "Tony, he asked me if I knew a 'Sergeant Naturale.' I told him I hadn't seen you for a while and then said please don't get me involved. I don't know who that guy was but I know he's a 'mob' guy." Around this time I was making quite a few gambling arrests and probably messing up their numbers operation.

I called my FBI contact and gave him the plate that I had gotten and told him about the incident. Very quickly he contacted me back and said, "You're right, he's a hit man, but don't worry, he's going to jail Friday for a long time for multiple murders." I had to remind him this was Wednesday and if he was going for many murders, one more wouldn't make much difference to him. He kind of chuckled and said, "Don't worry, Tony, we'll have you and your family covered until he's put away."

Well, I'm here many years later, so I guess they did their job. By the way, "Skins" went to jail for life and is still in.

I don't know if this is related to this guy or not, but a couple of weeks later another incident occurred. It was a Sunday morning and I had to go in to work. My wife and kids were leaving for church and she found a very large knife stuck in our front door. Amazingly enough, she didn't call me, she called her father and he immediately came over. She explained to me later that she didn't know if I was busy or not, that's why she called him. Well, they did eventually call me and I quickly came and checked the area, and of course dusted the knife for prints. The strange thing was there were no prints. The knife had been wiped clean.

I think it was actually a scare tactic. She was quite frightened because her friend Marie told her a knife in the door like that was a sign of the Mafia. Well, if it was a scare tactic it certainly worked on my wife. Needless to say, her father was a house guest for quite a few days while I was working nights.

CHAPTER 14

PROMOTED TO LIEUTENANT AND
POLICE ACADEMY

AFTER SIX YEARS as a Sergeant, I was promoted to Lieutenant and assigned back into the Detective Bureau. Not only did I have charge of gambling but I was also made the first Internal Affairs Officer for the Township of Montclair. Both the Gambling and Internal Affairs were firsts for Montclair. I don't know why they were always making me a first. I had no records to work with so I had to start my own. It wasn't an easy job, considering I had no help. I was able to take any detective I wanted as needed, so that helped.

Around the same time another first came my way. It was teaching a one-day physical fitness course at the police academy. The students were all older officers, mostly Lieutenants, Captains, etc. Now I was talking about ten minutes and I noticed most of the guys weren't paying much attention and were half-asleep. From my sitting position I jumped on top of the desk and was now standing up on the desk. This was just an impulse move, not anything I planned.

It seemed to work. They all looked up. Their eyes were fixed on me. From that position I continued my spiel. Everyone was now fully awake.

The whole class was very attentive after that. And at the end of the class many of them came up to me and started asking questions about fitness. I guess they wondered how a forty-plus-year-old man could jump up like that. Who was it who said white men can't jump?

One of the students hung around while everyone left. He didn't look like a cop to me. He had a pad in his hand and seemed to be taking notes. He came up to me and said, "I'm from the New Jersey State Education Committee for Police Academies." I thought to myself, now I was really in trouble for jumping on the desk. To my surprise he started asking me how I did it. I explained to him that I could always jump but never had done it before and just did it on impulse. He then asked me if I could do it any time. Sure, I said. I had to do it for him again and again, probably five or six times, and did it very easily. "Okay," he said, "now how would you like to teach here on a regular basis to the new police cadets? But I would want you to include your desk jump. I think you would really get their attention by doing that. After all, if they see a man your age staying in shape, they will want to also."

Actually I was still in pretty good shape and worked out pretty regularly. Today, at age seventy-two, I still do 400 sit-ups daily (200 in the morning and 200 at night) and 50 push-ups. In fact, for my fiftieth birthday they gave me a heavy punching bag; on my sixty-fifth birthday they gave me "The Chuck Norris Gym," and on my seventieth, a set of weights. Who knows what I'll get for my eightieth (if I'm still around)?

I accepted the job and the gentleman from the state was right. The first thing I did before each class started was jump on my desk. In the beginning, they all thought I was a crazy old man but as the classes progressed, they seemed to get into it.

Another thing I had them do, when they had a coffee

break, was break the donut in half and only have a half-cup of coffee, explaining that they would only have one-half the amount of calories. Believe it or not, most all of them did it. Once in a while I still see some of my recruits. They all seem to remember me, especially my "table trick." Some of them called me the "Half-Donut Lieutenant." Many of them ask me if I still do the table jump.

Actually, I do. I've been doing it at weddings for years and I just recently did it at my fiftieth class reunion. I had to do it three times because some of my classmates had missed it. My wife went nuts because she leaves the room every time I do it. She was going in and out of the restroom like crazy. Everyone thought she had the "runs." She said she doesn't want to see me break my neck. Gee, maybe she does love me. I guess I'm just a physical fitness nut. Well, a nut, anyway.

If you recall, when I was tricked into joining the Navy, the recruiter stated I would go to college free. Well, he was right. At age forty-and-a-half, I enrolled in Montclair State College, taking Police Science courses under the LEAP (Law Enforcement Education Program). In fact, a few of us had our picture taken with the local assemblyman Richard Codey, who sponsored the bill.

One of the courses was Forensic Science. This is the study of trace clues such as blood, fibers, hair, etc. While I was going to school at night, I was still assigned to the Detective Bureau during the day. At this point in time there wasn't much known about Forensic Science, and I must admit I knew nothing about it either. While I was working in the Detective Bureau, we had what they had classified as a double suicide (mother and daughter), who were found hanging in the cellar of their home. I saw in the Detective Bureau a pile of clothes and shoes on one of the chairs. I inquired about them and was told by a supervisor that they were from the suicides. I asked if they were going to be sent to the Forensic Lab of the State Police. He didn't seem to know what I was talking about, so I asked him if I could do it. "Sure," he said, "no problem." The items were then sent to the lab. In the meantime the husband/father of the two women was raising quite a stink, stating he believed they were murdered and did not commit suicide. They were found in their cellar, each hanging separately from an overhanging beam. He even had an article put in the *Reader's Digest* claiming they were murdered and the Police Department was negligent in the investigation. In the meantime, the shoes that came back from the State Police Lab positively showed the bodies had been moved, and then hung from the cellar beams. It seemed that the dirt and dust on the bottom of the shoes was different than that from the cellar floor.

With this information it was obvious that the bodies had been moved and it could not be suicide. Our investigation intensified but about a week or so later, we got a big break. A window washer was arrested in another town for murdering an elderly woman in her home. Our investigators went there and questioned him. He admitted doing our job. He was washing the windows at our victims' house, murdered them both, then took them to the cellar and hung them to make it look like suicide. Ironically, he was questioned about the women in the early part of the investigation but provided an alibi. This took a lot of pressure off the town because the victims' husband/father was getting ready to sue the town.

Well, I completed my course, got my college degree within four-and-a-half years, and was able to maintain a 3.0 average. After the first two years I changed my major to education. I figured this would be more beneficial to me after I retired. It wasn't easy but I also got my teaching certificate. I must say I would never have graduated if it wasn't for my wife, who typed all my papers. The big problem was I didn't write too legibly. I would leave her my notes, go to work and she would type them. Many times, I would be in the middle of an interrogation and she would call me on our "hot line" and very loudly say, "Anthony, I can't read your damn writing." Well, needless to say, this caused a lot of laughs among some detectives and even some prisoners. One such time after she called, saying the same thing all the time, a wise-guy prisoner we were questioning obviously heard her, and said to me, "Anthony, I would like to go back to my cell block."

Oh well, we only had to put up with my studies for about four years. My wife went through hell those four years and when I got my diploma, I told her it was half hers.

One thing I can't forget about Montclair State College was the party my wife had for me when I graduated. Now remember this, I was forty-five years old, so I knew a lot of people. We had about 200 people there and it was July and very hot. Everyone seemed to gather on the porch. The party was really going when my daughter, LeeAnn, who was only about 120 pounds, walked onto the porch. It suddenly caved in; boards actually split and some of the people fell through to the ground.

Actually it was quite funny because no one got hurt and now people still say, "Remember when Tony graduated and his porch caved in?" One thing most of them didn't know was that I had just repaired the porch the day before, replacing some old rotted planks. Well, I never claimed to be a carpenter anyway. Now my wife won't let me fix anything. (I'm not so dumb.) She says, "Remember when you fixed the porch and it caved in?" How could I forget? I'm sure not too many forty-five-year-old college graduates remember the highlight of their graduation being the collapse of their front porch.

While I was working on a gambling operation, I had a young detective assisting me. We sometimes used his private vehicle. We would always change cars for better surveillance. It was cheaper than renting cars (like some departments did). We would fill the tank up at the town garage and be on our way.

Now the story I'm about to tell played a big part in helping eliminate a certain group that was holding up banks to finance their political beliefs. They would not stop at murder and they in fact did kill one of our Sergeants who had been guarding the bank that they robbed. They also killed the retired Sergeant who was my boss mentioned earlier.

We heard a report of a hold-up in progress at the bank in Montclair Center. Naturally everyone converged to that area. We were getting descriptions of the perpetrators over our radio when Peggy Thomas, one of the meter maids (who was on our radio channel) said she saw someone walking on Willow Street who seemed to fit the description. We were right there, so we started to approach him, when two marked radio cars pulled up in front of us. The young detective wanted to jump out and help, but I said, "Hold on, there's enough men there, we'll just stand by."

They didn't even see us in the little Volkswagen. So we watched while they checked him out. After a few minutes, to my surprise, they let him go and pulled away. He started walking away, down Bloomfield Avenue. I told the detective to follow him, but not too close. He said, "What for? He must be okay as they checked him out."

I said, "Just follow him."

As he was walking away he kept looking back. We followed him for less than a quarter of a mile and even the new detective thought he looked suspicious by now. We jumped out at him just before the town line and immediately held him. He was quite surprised. He said, "Hey, Car Thirteen just checked me out and let me go—what are you doing?"

I noticed he had two sets of clothing on and his answers to our questions were very evasive. We immediately cuffed him and brought him to headquarters. In the meantime they apprehended two others who fit the descriptions.

The FBI was called in. They had jurisdiction over this case. For hours the one we brought in kept denying his involvement. Finally one of them cracked and implicated the one we brought in. Eventually I learned the one we brought in talked to the agents and involved many others that were part of the group. This arrest was very instrumental in diminishing this political group. The funny thing is the FBI got most of the credit. I really didn't care. The main thing is many bank jobs were cleared and put a big dent in the political group.

After that job, the young detective looked forward to working with me. He was very honest and I used him whenever I could on my Internal Affair jobs.

I have to include this story about the young detective, Phil Wagnor. When he first came on the job, he would sometimes work on my shift. The first night I had him, we were at an accident scene. During the investigation I could see him eyeing me pretty closely. I figured he was observing me to learn the ropes. Slowly he approached me and whispered in my ear, "Sergeant, your fly is open." Well, I guess he was pretty observant. He was right; it was open. I think he'll make a good investigator.

The next job with him wasn't an Internal Affairs job, but a routine arrest. First I have to give you some background on some events that were happening over the previous few months. We had two murders in the same apartment on Orange Road. The strange thing about this was that both were elderly women, both were murdered and then raped . . . not raped and then murdered. People were getting more than anxious in the area, especially when it was discovered that the tenant before these two also was discovered dead in the exact same apartment about a year earlier. Although her death was deemed natural at the time, it was now being looked into further as a possible homicide.

Just about everyone was used in this investigation. I was even used to interrogate witnesses. It was just too coincidental that these murders and the alleged natural death were not related. We were getting a lot of publicity on this and the pressure was on to solve them. The Deputy Chief in charge of the investigation formed a special squad, and along with the Prosecutor's detectives, that's all they worked on.

It's ironic that the big break came not from the special squad, but from the new detective who worked with me. He was investigating an arrest of a peeping tom. When I came in, he said, "Lieutenant, look at this arrest report of a peeping tom we had during the night."

After I read the report, I informed him to take the arrest report right over to the special squad handling the murders. Those detectives intensively questioned him and he eventually admitted to the murders. He was a cab driver and would drive these women home late at night, wait outside the apartment until he figured they were asleep, then break in, kill them and then rape them. It was believed that he even did the first alleged natural death. Everyone was very relieved and all involved did a great job, especially the young detective. A detective magazine picked up the story and published it. We were all relieved and so were the citizens of Montclair.

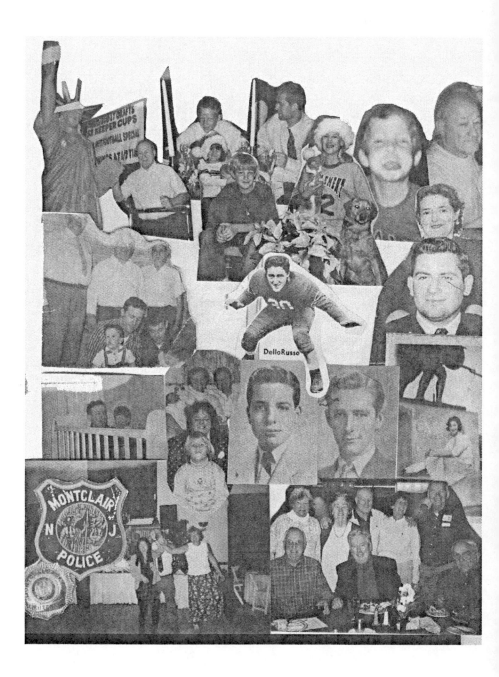

7399 141 GORDONHURST AVE., UP. MTCLR.

7

CHAPTER 15

THE JUVENILE BUREAU

SOMEWHAT LATER I was transferred to the Juvenile Bureau.

Now when I arrived there, the Captain in charge was very apprehensive because I was still in Internal Affairs. I could hardly blame him, because here I was working for him and many times I would have to run out, and naturally I couldn't tell him where or why. It wasn't a good situation and he would sometimes think I was planted there to spy on him or his men. I explained to him many times that wasn't the case. He was a very honest man and did a great job with the juveniles. He was, however, a bit paranoid and this didn't help the situation.

I did enjoy the Juvenile Bureau (JB), and the Captain and I got along very well. It was, however, like walking on eggs, because I had to leave so many times.

The juvenile job was very rewarding. You actually helped people rather than arrest them. There were times we would have to send some to the youth house but that was usually for a short period of time.

The most prominent case that comes to mind is the case of—we'll call him T. Now, I met T just a few days after I got into the JB. He was really a likeable kid but he was messed up. T had observed his father shoot and kill his mother when he was very young. He was placed with his grandmother (who lived in Montclair) soon after the incident. T also got along well with the Captain. We both liked him and tried to help him as much as possible. Because I had more time to come and go, the Captain more or less allowed me to take T under my wing and guide him.

I want to tell you he was the most "street smart" kid I ever encountered. If you allowed it, he would con you to death. I would get him little jobs to keep him off the street. Through the town, I got him a job to paint the house numbers on the curbs. He would get so much per house. I would drop him off in an area and then pick him up later during the day. This one day, I came by a little earlier and I saw three young boys in the area where T was supposed to be working. I inquired about T and they said, "Oh, we work for T."

I said, "How much does he pay you?"

It seemed T was quite an entrepreneur. He was giving them one-half of what he was getting and he would go to the store and sip sodas all day. We straightened that out. I made him give the correct amount and informed him he couldn't do that. The job was his if he wanted it, but he would have to do the work. "Okay," he said, "but I have to fire my two guys."

"Fine," I said.

At night T would get in some kinds of trouble and I would try and straighten him out during the day. We eventually did straighten him out and I have to say my wife helped with this. She was a secretary in the school where he went, and one time he was in the office threatening office workers with a small knife. She very calmly walked up to him and said, "T, give me that knife. What do you think you're doing?"

He very calmly handed her the knife and said, "Mrs. Natch, you're not going to tell your husband, are you?"

"Well, T, I've already called him and he's on his way."

When I got there he was very apologetic and started telling me his problems he was having with his grandmother. I started checking some of the things that he complained about, and it seemed some of it was true. Apparently she was getting Social Security money for him and it was to be used on his clothing and other necessities, and she wasn't doing this. The Captain was able to rectify this and T reacted much better after that.

Now the beauty of this story is this: T joined the Air Force when he turned eighteen. The first year he was in, he got married. He called me at my home when he got married. He called me again when he had his first child. After I retired (he had to be about thirty years old then), I got a call from him on Christmas Day. He told me he had another child and that he was out of the service and was a "Bounty Hunter." Wow—some of the people in town wouldn't believe it, but I did. He really straightened out and his record had to be clean to carry a gun. What really pleased me was when he said, "Lieutenant, you really straightened me out. If it wasn't for you, I would never have made it." He even offered me a job as a Bounty Hunter. I said, "No thanks, T," but I appreciated the gesture.

He continues to call me and still informs me about his family. Oh, incidentally, he's the young boy that I had mentioned earlier who gave me all that information from the streets.

Another case that worked out well while in the JB was the arrest of many juveniles smoking pot in front of the high school. We had gotten a complaint from school officials stating they were finding many roaches (spent marijuana butts) on the steps of the Amphitheater. We had to find a surveillance spot so I went to the janitor of George Inness School (across the street) and he gave me a key to the roof. It was a perfect spot; with binoculars I could watch from across the street. We placed detectives on the street and as I watched them come out and light up, I would describe them to the detectives. They would pull up and make the arrest. We were able to utilize this for about one week and made many arrests, and we never had any more complaints from the high school.

There were numerous cases in the JB and they were very rewarding. I was only there two years but the memories are very vivid.

While I was there I worked mostly days so I had time at night to work. I couldn't do much electrical work at night so I did a few jobs with a friend of mine, Tom Athill. Tom's parents came from Bermuda and Tom was born here. He was a good friend for many years. I hooked up Tom with Frank because Tom also was an electrician. So when we stopped doing alarms, Frank started working with Tom, doing electrical work. The three of us worked together on many electrical jobs and we would laugh the whole time.

Tom loved police work and I know he would have loved to be a policeman, but it didn't work out. He did, however, join the County Reserves and did see some action there.

Now the night work that I was referring to was with Tom. He got tied up with National Car Rentals, looking for stolen cars. Tom was good at this, but he wasn't a policeman and he didn't carry a gun. That's where I came in. He hired me and we would go looking for stolen cars. We would spot the car and use a master key to get into it and another master key for the ignition to start. Tom had a machine that could make keys right on the spot. A lot of the cars were just ones that people wouldn't return on time. Tom would usually take care of these himself. Sometimes it was a matter of just improper paperwork. Most of these cars were ones the persons would rent and just not return. However, I would assist him on the more difficult ones where there was usually no intention of returning. That's the ones we would go after.

We would work it this way. If it was a white policeman on the desk I would go in, explain it to the Desk Officer, show him our paperwork, and he would say okay. If it was a black Desk Officer, Tom would go in and do the same. It always went smoother that way.

Here is what happened this one night. We had to go to Harlem and we spotted the car before we were able to notify the police. We parked a couple of cars behind it and Tom got out and went to a telephone to call the police for assistance, because the guy was still in the car. I was sitting in the car behind him, waiting for assistance. Suddenly the guy started the car up and attempted to pull out. I had to do something or he was gone. I quickly pulled right up alongside him and blocked him in. He jumped out of the car. I figured he was going to run or fight. I jumped in front of him and yelled, "Stop, Police."

Now I'm not exaggerating when I tell you this guy was big. He was about six-foot-six and probably 300 pounds. When I saw this, I quickly held out my Police badge (not the National Car Rental badge) and opened my jacket so he could see my weapon. He just looked at me but didn't move. It seemed like fifteen minutes we waited and stared at each other (actually it was about three minutes) and all of a sudden here came a New York Sergeant, a couple of his men and Tom. Boy, did they look good to me. Actually, many people had gathered around us and I was the only white face in the crowd, except for the Sergeant. The NYC Sergeant said to me, "What the hell are you doing here? Are you crazy or something?" He was shaking his head as he read the prisoner his rights and informed him he was under arrest.

When we got to the Police Station, the prisoner realized we were car rental cops. He yelled, "You mean I was arrested by 'Rent-a-Cops'?" Boy, was he hot. Good thing he was behind bars at the time. We found out why he was so upset. He was wanted in numerous states for auto theft. The next day when he was being arraigned, two Brooklyn detectives came and told the judge that he was wanted for murder in their Borough. He was going to spend a lot of time in jail.

I also remember this case very vividly because this is the first time "The Godfather" was seen on TV. We all watched it together in the precinct while we were doing the paperwork, but he was behind bars. Every once in a while we could hear him muttering, "Damn, arrested by Rent-a-Cops." It was a long night but a good movie.

Well, Tom and I had many close ones. One time, a man came running out of his house in his underwear as we were pulling away with his rental car. Thinking we were car thieves, he began firing a shotgun at us. Obviously, he must have called the police as we got stopped before we got through the Lincoln Tunnel. After showing the paperwork, we were sent on our way. The guy wasn't a very good shot, thank God. We could probably write a book on just our "Car Rental" episodes.

Tom has remained a good friend and we still chat about "old times" now and then.

Also while I had nights off I was able to help coach Midget Football with the Montclair Cobras, run by Howard Finney Jr.; his father had started the Cobras many years before and Howard continued it. It was getting to be too big a job for one person so Howard had asked me to help, and being my son Steven and nephew Richard were playing on the team, I felt that I wanted to help. It was a great experience. Howard was a very dedicated person and he is still doing it today. Now he has a few coaches to help out and has more than one team.

One incident sticks out for me while I was coaching with the Cobras. We traveled to Nebraska one year to play a Nebraska team. By now, Skippy Rizzie was also assisting coaching. The boys all slept with Nebraska boys and the coaches were in a hotel. It must have been about three AM and Skippy woke me up and said he was really sick. He had had a couple of beers so I said, "Just take a couple of aspirin and go to sleep." But he wouldn't; he kept bugging me, saying he was really sick. "Okay, I'll call the desk and see if they can get a doctor." I did and they gave me a doctor's number. I gave it to Skip and told him to tell him his problem.

I heard Skip say, "Yes, yes, okay." Then he hung up. Then he lay down.

I said, "Wait a minute. What did he say?"

He turned over towards me and said, "He said take a couple of aspirin and go to sleep."

Wow, maybe I missed my calling.

The Cobras lost the game to Nebraska 6-0. Thirty years-plus and Howard Finney still coaches the Cobras.

Now I'm trying to keep everything in chronological order, but this is almost impossible over the amount of years I'm covering. At this point I'm a Lieutenant in the Juvenile Bureau but there are a couple of things I want to include when I was patrolman. My wife, in fact, reminded me of this humorous incident that occurred my first day alone on a post. We were working the four-to-midnight shift, and the uptown radio car officer was letting me off at Bellevue and Valley Roads. It had been raining a little and I had the long "cape-like" raincoat on. The patrolman stopped, let me off and then slowly pulled away. To his surprise, he saw me running alongside the police car and saw me waving to him. (No, I didn't have to go to the bathroom.) This went on for a short distance and then he finally heard me yell, "Stop!" So he stopped and I reached over and opened the door.

He said, "Tony, what the hell are you running alongside of the car for?"

I said, "Ed, my raincoat was caught in the door and it was either run or get dragged, so I decided to run." We both started to laugh.

He said, "I knew you were in pretty good shape and figured you just wanted to run for exercise."

For many years he told that story and always got a good

laugh. This patrolman eventually became Chief of the Department.

The other thing was when I was riding the three-wheel motorcycle. Actually during this period of time I was riding the two-wheel cycle for a couple of days and then three days on the three-wheeler. It did become confusing at times. On one the bar-shift was a clutch and the other it was the brake. This particular day, I was on the three-wheeler. A truck driver had stopped and hailed me down. I slowly headed towards his large truck. As I got near it I hit what I thought was the brake, but it wasn't—it was the clutch, and I went faster and banged hard into the side of the truck. The astonished driver looked down at me and yelled, "Christ, all I wanted was directions."

Well, no real damage was done and we both got a good laugh from it.

Because of the next story I want to insert this information about policemen. Statistics prove they have the most divorces, the most heart attacks and the most suicides among all professions. Well, heart attacks, I'm sure you can understand. You go from a very relaxed position sitting in an auto, to running from the auto at full exertion, chasing someone or running into a house in an attempt to save someone, and constantly wrestling with someone. This is a strain on your heart. Divorces I also can understand, because you are away so much, all types of hours, and there are many more temptations than the average job. I really don't understand the suicides, except there are so many highs and lows, I guess it's easier to get depressed.

Anyway, I was a Sergeant at this time and one patrolman seemed very depressed. We talked a few times and he told me about his wife running off with another man. Actually, he still did his job, and very well, so I guess he covered up his depression pretty well. I told him he should try and forget it, but maybe he should seek some professional help. He promised me he would. A couple of days later (I was off), he went to his post in the radio car and after about an hour on the tour, they attempted to get a hold of him and couldn't. A search was made and they found him in his radio car, dead of an apparent self-inflicted gunshot wound. This was very unfortunate because he was still a young man and had two young children.

While I was on the job I believe we had four suicides. Not only did the families have to endure the complexities of the job, now they had to endure this. I would say policemen's families sometimes suffer more than the police themselves.

While in the Juvenile Bureau, I instituted a "log." This log showed what detective was working what case. I couldn't believe the way it was done prior to the log. Cases would be put on specific detectives' desks and piled up. If someone had to add to the case, they would have to search each detective's desk. This was such a simple thing, I don't know why no one thought of it before. I'm very proud to say they are still using the log in both the Detective and Juvenile Bureaus, and it has been installed into a computer program.

As a Lieutenant in the Juvenile Bureau I was able to log a lot of hours on the road, partly because of my Internal Affairs duties and also because you really didn't need two supervisors in the Juvenile Bureau all the time. At this point in time I no longer was doing gambling enforcement, but sometimes things just occur and you can't overlook them.

I had arrested this store owner on Bloomfield Avenue. We'll call him "C." I had arrested him twice, and the second time he served some time in jail. While he was in jail, his store had been condemned for health violations and was supposed to be closed. He had just gotten out and as I was riding by I saw him serving customers. I immediately stopped and went in and inquired about his actions. Well, he gave me some excuse and I chased the customers out and informed them of the status of the store. Even though I had arrested him twice and had him put in jail, he thanked me for not arresting him now.

As he got closer to me, I saw a big pad sticking out of his pocket and very visibly, I could see "numbers slips" also sticking out of his pocket. Now, I had been doing this for many years and I knew these were illegal numbers slips. I said, "Mr. C, I don't believe you are still dealing with numbers." He started to plead his case but I couldn't overlook this. I started to place him under arrest. He pulled a wad of bills out of his pocket (obviously the numbers money) and said, "Here, take this money, it's yours. I can't go to jail again."

I said, "Just a minute, Mr. C, I can't take that money, I don't cover this post anymore, but let me get the guys who do cover it, okay?"

"Sure," he said.

So I called the radio car that covered the area and two young patrolmen arrived. "What's up, Luke [Lieutenant]?" they asked.

I said, "Mr. C has something for you."

Now he started to hand them the big wad of bills and they looked at me very quizzically, one of them stating, "We can't take that, Lieutenant."

I said, "Go ahead, it's okay," giving them a slight wink. Very reluctantly they took it.

Firmly, I said, "Okay, now I want you to count it, date it, and mark it as evidence, then place Mr. C under arrest for possession of numbers slips and bribery."

Both men felt very relieved because they were both very honest men and they probably believed, for a time, that the Internal Affairs Officer was going bad.

Mr. C went to jail for possession of illegal numbers and bribery and as he was in his seventies at the time, will probably be in the rest of his life. Just to the right of Mr. C, when he was arrested, was a box with a newspaper on top of it. Under the paper was a fully loaded .38 pistol. We found out later that Mr. C was ready to shoot and kill me if I arrested him again. Fortunately for me, he was never in the position to get to the weapon.

CHAPTER 16

COMMANDER OF THE

DETECTIVE BUREAU

WELL, AFTER THE Juvenile Bureau, I was sent back to the Detective Bureau. Captain Valenti, who was in charge, made Deputy Chief, and as a Lieutenant I was put in charge of the Investigative Section of the Detective Bureau. The Chief made a bunch of young guys detectives and they were really sharp. They actually made me look good. We didn't have any unsolved cases when I left. The fact that just about every one of them have moved "up the ranks" proved that they were good men. One of the Sergeants from our unit made Chief. When he retired, one of the young detectives, Dave Harman, made Chief. He, in fact, became the first black Chief of Police for the Township and as of this writing is still the Chief.

One murder case sticks out in my mind. In fact, it was the last one I was in charge of before I went back to the Uniform Division.

An elderly man was murdered on Orange Road. It seems he surprised a burglar in his home and was stabbed numerous times. The case was at a standstill and I figured I would check with an informant I used who lived in the area. We questioned him about it (because he was a burglar) and he said he knew the old man but had no ideas on who may have done it.

After a few weeks he never came back to me with any info, so I asked him if he would be willing to take a lie detector test, just to eliminate him. I told him this was just routine. He agreed. Every time we scheduled it he had an excuse. Finally I called him up and said, "Look, we'll pick you up today because our lie detector man is here now." He said okay. The detectives went to pick him up at his apartment and his girlfriend said he took off right after speaking to me. That did it. We got a "consent warrant" to search the apartment and the detectives found a credit card from the murdered man in the pocket of my informant's jacket hanging in the closet. That nailed it down. An arrest warrant was issued for his arrest and he was apprehended shortly thereafter. When he was apprehended he gave a statement admitting his guilt.

One of the detectives involved in his arrest, Dave Harman, became Chief a few years later, and as I had previously stated, became the first black Chief for the Township of Montclair, and still holds that position as of this writing. The other detective, Rocco Miscia, a very bright detective, took over my job as Internal Affairs Officer after I retired. In fact, a third detective who worked for me, Errol Brudner, rose to the rank of Captain, has just recently retired and became head of Safety and Security at the same local hospital, the same job I had a few years earlier. Rocco Miscia also became a Captain and just recently retired.

I didn't remain in charge of the Detective Bureau very long. We moved from upstairs and the whole building was revamped. I was there during the change and there was much more security and cameras throughout the building. I was transferred to the Uniform Division and became the day

Watch Commander. Actually this was a much easier job because I had a Sergeant and a Lieutenant working for me on the same tour, and additionally it was an eight-to-four job so I was off evenings. I would make out the schedules and then tour the streets. I would go on as many calls as possible but it seemed while you were uptown, the calls would be downtown and vice-versa. Soon I learned to stay in the center area so I could hit most calls.

I was now fifty-seven years of age, and was in my second year as Watch Commander when I started to think about retiring. As Watch Commander you're not usually the first one on a call but this one day, I was. It was downtown on New Street and the call was a "disturbance" on the street. As I approached I saw a large crowd. This was odd because it was only about ten AM. I jumped out of my car and came upon a young boy, about sixteen, holding a knife against another boy's throat. I approached him slowly, asking him to let the boy go and to give me the knife. He yelled, "Stay away from me or I will kill him!" I kept getting closer and closer and held both my hands out so he could see I had no weapon in my hands. Two other policemen approached with their weapons out and I instructed both to holster their weapons, which they did.

I was now within a few feet and he let go of the boy and started swinging the knife towards me. It seemed that he had been crying and it appeared that he was high on something. I looked him straight in the eye and asked him for the knife, informing him that no one would hurt him. His response to this was to swing the knife at me, just narrowly missing my outstretched hand.

Now you're not going to believe this, but what went through my mind was that he almost hit my left hand, my pitching hand, and I had to pitch that night (softball). Actually this angered me a little and I made a lunge for his hand with the knife, grabbing the knife and his hand, and quickly was able to knock him to the ground, twisting his arm behind him. The two patrolmen then came to my assistance and we cuffed and arrested him.

I had the rest of the tour to think about this and finally decided that I was getting too old to wrestle with eighteen-year-old kids in the prime of their life. Besides, if he cut my hand, that may be the end of my softball days. I talked it over with my wife and we both decided it was a good idea to retire. I turned in my papers the very next day and, after thirty-four years, was no longer a policeman.

CHAPTER 17

RETIREMENT TIME

THIS ISN'T THE end of my story . . . the *police* end of it, but there was still much more to come in my unbelievable life. A big part of my life was softball. I started playing when I first joined the Police Department. We used to play "fast pitch" and play other Police Departments. It was a lot of fun then because the wives and kids would come, and after the games we would have sandwiches and pizza and soda. There was a great camaraderie then among all the departments, and we would actually discuss cases. Many times we could actually clear some jobs through our conversations. Sometimes we would argue and even fight.

One such time we were playing the Newark Police at Schools Stadium on Bloomfield Avenue. One of our guys, Richard, accidentally spiked Bruno, the Newark first baseman, as he crossed the bag. They both were pretty high-tempered guys and before we knew it, they started fighting. Both benches emptied and soon everyone was fighting. Someone very wisely called the police. Hey, we *are* the police; where did all these other guys come from? Anyway, eventually it all became calm and we completed the game. We still all went for food and drinks and everyone remained friends. I don't remember who won the game.

I also played in many town leagues and am still playing after fifty years. At this point my wife no longer comes to my games, and of course my kids have their own kids' games to attend.

In one town game, I think I was the oldest guy (about sixty), and one of the young guys on the team (about twenty-one) had pulled a muscle as he ran to first. I had made the last out so I had to run for him. I was on first and an elderly gentleman looked at me very strangely and said, "Tony Naturale, is that you?"

Well, of course it was me, and I said, "Yes, it's me."

He said, "That's my grandson you're running for. What the hell, you still playing? I played with you about thirty years ago."

I remembered; I didn't have Alzheimer's yet, and yes, I was still playing.

I will go into more about softball and the Senior Olympics a little later, but first things first.

I just retired from the Police Department and was getting ready for a new job. I was off all of three days and then started my job as Director of Safety and Security at a local hospital. Actually I had gone for an interview a few months prior to retiring. I really didn't think I would retire yet and didn't think I would even be considered for the job. There were numerous applicants and some were really good. Many of the applicants had Master's degrees, and with my Bachelor's degree I didn't think I had a chance. It turned out what put me over the top was my electrical experience. That knowledge sure did help me and even with that, I still had to take a three-month course at Essex County College for State Inspector and had to get a State License. I was responsible for all the Fire Safety Training and all the inspections throughout the hospital. Nineteen hundred employees had to be trained yearly.

The first thing I did was hire a Montclair fireman, part-time, to assist me with inspections. I eventually turned all inspections over to him. This was a tremendous responsibility and took a big load off of me. Next I hired a retired police officer, Richard Tait. He had been appointed to the Police Force the same day as me. We became good friends and remained that way throughout our respective careers. He also retired as a Lieutenant and was quite a baseball player. He, in fact, had played with Mickey Mantle in the minor leagues and would probably have made it further if he hadn't injured his arm. He was the big star on our softball team and probably the reason we were so good. I hired Richard at the hospital and he did a great job stationed at the emergency ward. He stood about six-foot-three and weighed about 230 pounds, and the main thing: he knew who the bad guys were. Once I hired him, I no longer had to go to the emergency room every time there was a problem. He handled it himself.

My first day on the job was a very active one. I had to speak at my first meeting and was introduced to all the other Directors and President and Vice-Presidents. Now I know you're not going to believe this (maybe by now you will), but as I went to my designated seat, I tripped over an electric cord going across the middle of the room. I stumbled very awkwardly towards my seat. Now I had something to talk about. Imagine this, the Safety Officer tripping on an electric cord. Well, that's kind of the story of my life. Nothing is normal. Oh well, it would be a very dull life if things didn't happen to me. Anyway, everyone got a good laugh out of it. I told everyone that my first job as the Safety Officer was to get rid of all electrical cords running across the floors. The meeting went quite well and every time I spoke at the meetings, I would inject a little humor into my spiel and it seemed to go quite well. (No, I didn't jump on any tables.)

I didn't realize how immense this job was. I was in charge of the safety and security of the entire hospital and had to train 1900 employees in fire safety. Hiring the policeman for the emergency room and a fireman for the inspections was probably the smartest thing I did, but overall getting cameras installed proved the safest. The hospital had no existing cameras and I put in for thirty cameras to be installed throughout the hospital. Eventually they approved for twenty-two cameras and I also had a monitor room installed. I didn't realize the power I had. It seemed that just about anything I asked for, I got. Of course, it didn't hurt that Lou Raccioppi was a Vice-President and my immediate supervisor. We had played together on the Montclair High School football team and had become friends. Also, most all other hospitals had security cameras so that made my request come easier.

Once I had the cameras installed and the monitor room set up, I hired a woman to monitor the cameras. This allowed my guards to move around and constantly check all floors all hours of the night. The nurses loved this because previously they would never see a guard during their entire shift. Every guard was instructed to check with the nurse on each floor at least twice a tour. It was being run more like a police tour and they seemed to feel safer. We also initiated having a guard walk the employees to their respective cars on the night shifts. I would come in all hours and check on the guards. In fact, in the first year I got rid of three guards who weren't doing their respective jobs.

Actually one of the things I'm most proud of while working at the hospital was doing the budget. I was actually able to reduce my budget each year I was there and even increase the number of guards.

Coming from the Police Department was really an asset for me. I knew who the bad guys were. I would walk the halls and knew who belonged in the hospital.

One day I observed a drug addict I had arrested numerous times. I didn't know what he had done but when he saw me, he ran from the hospital. I immediately got a guard and with the van, we drove to his home address. We waited while he walked from the hospital, thinking he had gotten away. We stopped him before he got to his house and found numerous items on him that he had stolen from the hospital. The funny thing about it was he thought I was still on the Police Department and thought I was just visiting the hospital. He learned otherwise when we called the Glen Ridge Police Department and had him arrested. I never saw him in the hospital again.

There were many internal thefts throughout the hospital, and this had to be addressed. My friend Frank and I installed a couple of "peephole" cameras in the hospital and we would move them around from time to time. The word got around but no one knew where they were. If a director was experiencing thefts within a particular department, I would be notified and we would install a "peephole" and it usually stopped. I recall one such case where the doctors' lockers and refrigerators were being entered. After one day with the camera, a worker was caught and immediately fired. The worker kept denying it but when we showed him doing it on the tape, he finally admitted to it.

A funny incident happened one day that was hard to forget. It seemed one particular doctor would constantly park his personal car in the emergency circle and leave it there for hours at a time. I received numerous complaints so I had the guards leave notices on the vehicle to refrain from parking there. This didn't work, so I called the Glen Ridge Police and had a summons put on the vehicle. This doctor called me to the emergency entrance and we had quite a discussion on it, but he must have paid the ticket because it wasn't contested. Anyway, a couple of days later, one of the guards, who was quite friendly with this doctor (who was a prostate specialist), said the doctor "would love to get Anthony Naturale on the operating table." Well, I just laughed it off because he wasn't my doctor and never will be after a comment like that.

Now here's the funny part; part of it, anyway. My cousin Joe Naturale passed away and I was at the funeral talking to his brother (my cousin), also named Anthony Naturale. He told me he was coming to our hospital for a prostate operation and his doctor was . . . that's right, the same doctor who wanted to get me on the operating table. When I told him the story, we all laughed. My cousin Anthony wasn't laughing as hard as the rest of us, but I told him to say he didn't know me. He said, "Sure, I'll say I never heard of Anthony Naturale." Well, the operation was successful and Cousin Anthony did leave with all of his parts.

Another security move was to change all existing locks in the hospital. This required the maintenance lock man to work under my control. There were no more master keys given out and all key requests had to be approved by me. This angered a few of the doctors, but it had to be done and eventually they realized the reasons this was done.

Doing the budget was a big part of the job. I have to say right now I knew nothing about the computer and had to do some fast learning. The Materials Management Department was right next to my office and was run by Jeff Welch. Jeff was a great guy and really knew his stuff. He was a great help to me, especially teaching me about the computer and the budget. Now his secretary, Carol Ricca, had the middle office between Jeff and me. She was his secretary but many people thought she might have been my secretary also because she was in the middle and was in my office many times helping me out. I don't know what I would have done without her because she got me out of many jams with the computer. She would also check with both Jeff and me at lunchtime and get us lunch numerous times. In fact, she introduced both Jeff and me to peanut butter and banana sandwiches. I had never heard of them before and she would make them at home and bring them to us for lunch. Boy, they were good. (I still have them from time to time.) Thanks, Carol; not just for the peanut butter sandwiches but for all the invaluable help you gave me. Carol is still at the hospital and everyone loves her. Since I've gotten my computer, I e-mail Carol every now and then and she has even gotten me some electrical jobs. Thanks again, Carol.

I would like to make a comment about Jeff. He was in pretty good physical shape and had observed me do my desk jump. After a few tries, he actually did it. A doctor friend, Phil, also saw this and wanted to try it. Well, would you believe it? After all these years when so many people saw me do it and had tried unsuccessfully, these two guys do it. I guess I'm not the only physically fit dummy after all.

After about four-and-a-half years, my new Vice-President approached me. She told me that everything was going great in the Security Department, so they no longer needed a Security Director. I was quite shocked, especially when she told me my last day would be this coming Friday (this was on a Wednesday). I was now sixty-one years of age and wanted to work at least until age sixty-two (this was six months away).

Well, I flatly told her I was not leaving in two days and this was probably illegal. She just laughed and said, "Well, your last day on the payroll will be Friday." I again stated I would not leave.

She called the personnel officer and he called me, stating he had no choice but to follow what the Vice-President said. I told him I was contacting my lawyer and would initiate a suit because this was age discrimination. He asked me what I wanted. I told him I wished to work until December, on my sixty-second birthday. I told him what I had done for the hospital since I came and how I had lowered the budget each year since I was there, and all the extra hours I had put in for the good of the hospital. He said he knew I did a good job but it was out of his control, and the hospital could not grant my unreasonable request. They had never given more than three weeks' pay to any departing employee, but he would present it to the President and get back to me.

He hung up and I don't think it was more than twenty minutes later that he called me back and said, "Tony, I can't believe it—he said okay. And you don't have to come in. You will be paid in full until you reach age sixty-two."

I said, "Thanks, Joe." By me getting that six extra months, it gave me a small pension (five years) from the hospital.

Now I was really retired—or was I?

CHAPTER 18

THE HANDY MEN—BOB & TONY

I ACTUALLY DIDN'T do anything for a couple of weeks. I was bored to death. All I did was play softball about three times a week. I still ran the co-ed hospital softball team, and I continued to do that after I left the hospital. I then started to do a few electrical jobs. I got so busy I asked my friend Bob McKeown if he wanted to help me. Bob and his wife, Marie (the knife-in-the-door Marie), were our good friends for many years. Madeline had gone to Immaculate Conception High with Marie and they became good friends.

So Bob and I started doing not only electrical work but all kinds of handyman work. We were going along pretty well. In fact, we were getting so much work we had to stop doing all the other work and went back to just electrical work. Thank God we stopped the other because we really weren't that good at the other work.

One time I remember we were sheetrocking a ceiling and Bob had the five-gallon can of ready-made plaster at the foot of the ladder. When he stepped off of the ladder, he stepped right into the open can and couldn't get his foot out. I was laughing so hard I couldn't help him. I was watching as he was struggling to pull his foot out. If it had been in any longer than it was, I think the plaster would have set and he would have been in real trouble.

After that job we took on less and less plastering and eventually stopped all other work. We really didn't make a lot of money but we had a lot of laughs. I even began to think I should take a movie camera with us on the jobs. We probably could have made a lot more money. The only problem was no one would believe the things that happened to us.

I just remembered another story. This time I was the brunt of the incident.

We were working at a Catholic Bishop's house and I was standing in the sink trying to change a fixture over the sink. I had to stand in the sink—a ladder wouldn't fit. As I reached up holding one of the wires, I grounded myself standing in the wet sink and jumped back and grabbed the water faucet (making it worse), turned the water on, and fortunately fell back from the jolt and fell to the ground. Bob stood in the background laughing and the Bishop, who had witnessed the whole incident, seemed to be praying. Well, his prayers were apparently answered because I was unhurt and the fixture fell to the ground, never breaking. I always felt if we weren't in a holy person's house I would have been seriously injured, maybe electrocuted. And the fixture would have broken.

It was the last time we worked in that house. He never called us back. I don't know why.

Well, all good things come to an end, and this ended kind of the same way I ended up in the Navy. Bob and Marie were taking a look at some houses at the Shore and asked us if we wanted to go for a ride. Well, we went for the ride and guess what? Yep—we ended up buying a house.

Well, this wasn't a four-year ride like the Navy; this ended up only two years. We each bought a house in Lakewood, New Jersey at the Four Seasons and basically the same thing happened as when I joined the Navy: We moved first. They didn't move for almost six months after us.

It really was a beautiful area, but we were so far away from all the kids and that didn't please my wife. Actually, I was traveling north four times a week for my softball and bowling. It seemed like all I was doing was traveling. I even played ball for a Toms River team in between. Sometimes I wouldn't see Madeline for two days. In fact, for a while we only had one car, so Madeline was stuck without a car for a while. The funny thing about the whole situation was, I moved because I thought that's what she wanted, and she said she thought it was what I had wanted. Neither one of us actually wanted to move. This was a perfect case of "lack of communication." You can bet when we moved to where we are now, we talked and talked and talked.

Now that we live in Wharton, New Jersey, I'm only twenty minutes from my ball field and about the same for my bowling. Madeline has a car and travels to see our kids and grandkids as often as she wants. Our daughter LeeAnn Hurley lives in Rockaway, about five minutes away. She and her husband, Pat Hurley, have three children: Katie, Ryan and Emily. We see them quite often. Ironically, our daughter Carolyn moved to the Shore about the same time we moved back, but we do go down there quite often to see her and her newborn baby, David, and her spouse, Kevin, and his son, Evan.

CHAPTER 19

SOFTBALL

I STATED EARLIER in the story that I would get into my softball. I've been playing softball since I was twenty-four years old. Actually, I started playing with the Police Department as a rookie. I've been playing ever since. In the beginning it was fast-pitch. All the Police Departments were playing against each other. They don't do that anymore and it's too bad, because a lot of information was passed on about criminal activity and there was a better camaraderie than there is today.

A play sticks out in my mind when we were playing the State Police in Verona Park. If you know the area, you know there's a lake there. Well, the lake was just behind the left fielder. One of their batters hit a ball over our left fielder's head (Mike) and he just kept going back for it until he ended up in the lake. We all just laughed so hard as the guy easily rounded the bases for a home run. Boy, Mike, that was some try.

I also played in the town league until I was sixty-two years old and playing with twenty-five-year-old kids. Then I found out about the seniors leagues (fifty-nine and over), so I started playing with them. I couldn't believe there were that many old guys still playing. I thought I was the only one. One guy on our team was eighty-six years old and still could hit the ball.

Of course, sometimes you get a guy who's starting to get a little senile and funny things happen. Did you ever see two guys arguing and both had bad hearing? Well, you didn't have to know how to read lips to know what they were saying. No one got too offended because they couldn't always hear what each other had said. We had very few arguments because of this.

One time a guy hit the ball and ran right up the line to third base. I tried to tell him he should be on first and he says, "Didn't I get a triple?" It's a lot of fun and a lot of laughs.

Then you get guys like Don, who is seventy-six years of age and runs, hits and throws like a forty-year-old. Of course, when his hat falls off you can see he's a little older than that, but he's in great shape.

The majority of the players are really good athletes and really great guys. I've made a lot of friends and hope to make a lot more if I can continue playing.

In the Senior Olympics I played for the sixty-year-olds. This was my first one. We played in Tucson, Arizona, in 1997; the sixty-fives in Orlando, Florida, 1999; the sixty-fives in Baton Rouge, Louisiana, 2001; and God willing I hope to play for the seventies, 2003 in Norfolk, Virginia. Each time we go, my wife usually goes with me and we make a vacation out of it, and stay more than the usual four days.

A funny thing happened while we were in Arizona. We were all sitting around the pool between games and I started talking to one our pitchers, Walter Maly. He introduced me to his wife, Mary Ellen. We looked at each other and both realized we were in Montclair High School together. In fact, I reminded Mary Ellen that while we were seniors and in the same class, I sent her a note asking her to go out with me. She said she didn't remember it and I then reminded her she turned me down. She didn't remember that either.

Boy, some impression I made. You don't have to worry about me, Walt.

Walt and Mary Ellen have become good friends of ours and I don't send her any more notes.

I have almost come up to the point of where I am today, and I really don't have enough pages to make a complete book, but you must remember I never wrote a book before. I think I will have to contact my friend Grange (Peggy) Rutan Habermann.

Now I must tell you I knew Grange a long time ago (as Peggy Rutan). She used to go out with my brother Junior (Victor). In fact, everyone thought they were going to get married. Actually, Grange caught the bouquet at our wedding, but she and Vic never did get married. (Guess that doesn't work.)

Well, anyway, I met Grange at Dorothy and Donald's house about a year ago. Grange and her husband, Rolf, were talking to me about my book that I told them I was attempting to write. Rolf explained to me how Grange was a writer and that she could probably help me. Well, Grange has been helping me ever since and I must say is very capable. Thanks, Rolf. She has guided me all the way to this point, even though for the past thirteen years she has interviewed over 400 luminaries of the jazz world for her book. I guess she needed a rest. Thanks, Grange.

When she was very young, Grange married the Caucasian jazz bebop pianist, Al Haig, who, because of his talent, was able to cross over and be accepted in the black musical world which included Charlie Parker, Dizzy Gillespie and Miles Davis, to name a few. Her marriage didn't last long; in fact, it only lasted eight weeks, because he isolated her and mentally and physically abused her. But thank God, she escaped from him because, a few years later, he remarried and beat this wife also, eventually killing her, was arrested for homicide, tried and found not guilty. Somehow the jury found him innocent.

In Grange's book, through an enormous amount of research and numerous interviews, this book will allow the reader to not only know about Al's contribution to the music but also be a member of the jury so they can decide for themselves. Was Al Haig guilty or innocent? But I won't go into any more of it. You be a member of the jury, and you decide. The name of the book is *Bebop Wife by Lady Haig, AKA Grange Rutan (The Wife No One Knew)*.

CHAPTER 20

SENIOR OLYMPICS

I HAD STATED earlier, I became involved with the Senior Olympics at age sixty-two. I had been playing with the over-thirty league and one of the ball players (who was older than me) told me about the Olympics. Carl (Nookie) Lombardi had played with Mickey Mantle in Triple-A baseball and was some athlete. I didn't even know there was an over-sixty league until he told me about it.

I went to Degman Field in West Orange and played with his team, run by Walt Maly and John Healy. I couldn't believe all these old guys were still playing. I thought Carl and I were the only ones. The first year I played with the Nutley team, I did quite well and in fact had eight home runs that were the most by any player on our team. In fact, I was asked to play on the All-Star team.

But let me tell you about the home runs. That's a lot of home runs to hit in softball, but I had a little help. We played in Nutley at the Hoffmann-LaRoche field. If you know that field, you know there is a steep hill in the right field area. I am a left-handed hitter, and that's where most lefties hit (right field). Many of the hits should have been, at the most, doubles, but because of the hill, the minute the ball hit in that area it would roll right down the hill and just kept going. You could almost walk around the bases. I guess you could say I had a lot of help.

From there I played in a couple of tournament games and then was asked to play on the Senior Olympics team representing New Jersey. This was quite a thrill. We traveled to Tucson, Arizona but lost all three games. Madeline and Marie and Bob came with us and we made quite a trip of it. At the end of all the events, all the athletes marched onto the field at Arizona State College. There were well over 10,000 athletes, men and women, marching across the field. Fifty states were represented and it was quite a sight to see. I never knew there were so many old athletes, but they all looked very fit. In fact, Jack Palance, the eighty-something-year-old movie actor, did his famous one-handed push-ups to the delight of all the fans.

That was 1997. The Senior Olympics is held every two years. In 1999 it was held in Orlando, Florida. I was fortunate enough to be made the captain of this team. We fared a little better, winning two games and losing one, but unfortunately didn't get to the finals. Madeline was unable to attend because her brother was very ill.

In 2001, when we traveled to Baton Rouge, I was no longer the captain of the team but I did much better personally, going nine for twelve, sharing the top batting average with my teammate Al. We did win two out of three but again just missed making the finals.

In June 2003 we are supposed to play in Norfolk, Virginia and this time I hope to be playing with the seventies group (God willing).

As of this writing I am working out with the New Jersey hardball team and if I get selected, will travel to St. Petersburg, Florida, which is held every November, for the Roy Hobbs Seniors World Series (fifty-nine and over).

Well, believe it or not, the book still isn't quite finished and I did go to Norfolk, Virginia, June 2003.

Unfortunately we again just missed getting a medal. We won three games and lost two, losing the second game in sudden death. The sixty-five team (Pizzutti's) did win a bronze medal and the seventy-fives New Jersey team, the Embers (Walt Maly and John Healy's team), won a silver medal.

Of course I felt just fortunate to even be playing, because I had a knee replacement in March and this was only two-and-a-half months later, and no one thought I would even make the trip, even my doctor. I was only going to be a defensive hitter but after the second game, our first baseman became ill and had to go home so I was his replacement. We were very discouraged when we lost, but as we were walking off the field one of the guys remarked, "Hey listen, guys, we're lucky just to be playing at this age. We'll be back in two years and win it." We left Norfolk, Virginia a very happy group of guys.

At the Senior Olympics, Norfolk, VA, 2003. Over 70's category.

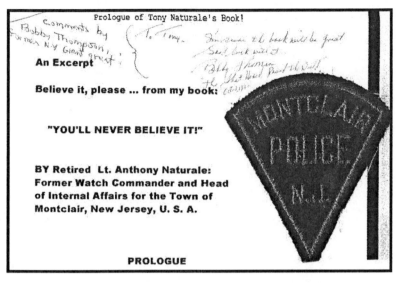

Comments by Bobby Thompson, former N.Y Giant great

An Excerpt

Believe it, please ... from my book:

"YOU'LL NEVER BELIEVE IT!"

BY Retired Lt. Anthony Naturale:
Former Watch Commander and Head
of Internal Affairs for the Town of
Montclair, New Jersey, U. S. A.

PROLOGUE

Bobby Thompson signed my book excerpt while we both
were recovering at Kessler's Institute in West Orange.

Below is a picture of Bobby hitting the famous home run,
"The Shot Heard Around the World" at the Polo Grounds
October 3rd 1951.

CHAPTER 21

COOPERSTOWN

AS I HAD previously stated, I was playing hardball once a week with a team Don Slocum had made up to play in Cooperstown, New York. I wasn't sure I could run the ninety feet at full speed after my knee replacement but after a few practices, I realized I could, so I started practicing with Don's team three times a week. On September 21, 2003 we went to Cooperstown with two teams assembled by him: the New Jersey Americans and the New Jersey Nationals. I started playing with the Americans but after the first game got switched to the Nationals.

Some really good players were there. Doc Pollak, a pitcher in the County leagues for many years, won the first game for the Nationals and he has the unbelievable record of almost 1,000 victories. At age sixty-eight, I'm sure he will surpass the 1,000 mark, as he only needs about five more victories. He also contributed with a .571 batting average. Don Slocum, at seventy-eight, was the oldest player on the field and finished up with a .471 average, and caught all the games. Jack McGroarty, a former Essex County police officer, was the defensive player of the series and also batted .461. John Pfander led all batters with a .777 average, followed by Frank Cavalarro with .583 and Jim Cupo with .545. Jamie Rivera contributed with a long home run and double and a .400 average.

Don Slocum's Nationals just missed winning the trophy, but a good time was had by all involved, especially this writer. We'll get them next year, guys; and thanks, Don Slocum, for doing a great job.

CHAPTER 22

THE ANIMALS

I CANNOT COMPLETE this book until I tell you about the animals in my life. It seems ever since I was a little kid we always had a dog, and if you remember way back in this story, it was my first encounter with the police, after my dog had been hit by a car. The dog was named King and he used to follow me everywhere. Everyone knew King; he even followed me to Mt. Hebron School one day and stood outside my classroom. He was like a member of the family and when he was run over and killed, our whole family was very saddened by it.

Well, probably our most memorable dog was Sultan. He was a very big Golden Retriever that we got from my good friends Pete Grout and Bobby (his wife). They loved dogs and cats and while Pete was a mailman, he picked up Sultan from one of his mail customers. It seemed they were having trouble with the dog and couldn't take care of him so Pete, who loved dogs, took him home. He knew we were looking for a dog at the time so brought him to us. We kept him and he was a great dog.

Let me tell you how great. Don't ask me how but I was

playing with him one day and noticed that every time I nodded my head he would bark. Now I started thinking hey, this is a smart dog, so I put up two fingers and very slightly nodded my head twice and he barked twice. Wow, I thought, this is pretty good, so I kept doing it every day and after he did it I would give him a cookie.

Now I was ready to try something with my wife and all the kids. I told them Sultan could count. Of course they didn't believe me. It worked every time. I even had him subtract by asking him to subtract with a certain amount of fingers. Of course any amount I wanted I would just slightly nod my head and he would bark. Everyone was looking at the dog, not at me, and wouldn't see my slight nod. We were becoming famous around the neighborhood. Everyone wanted to see Sultan add and subtract.

One instance really was funny. We had a guy who used to hang around the Plaza (Buzzy); he liked a few drinks now and then, and every time I would run through the Plaza with Sultan he would stop me and have me make Sultan count for him. One evening about seven p.m. he was on the corner at the Plaza, and a New York bus pulled up and passengers were getting off. Sultan and I were just coming up to the bus stop and Buzzy stopped me. He also stopped the passengers getting off the bus and literally held them back until I got there. He had announced to the small group of people that I had a very smart dog that could count and even add and subtract. Some of them knew Buzzy and figured he just had a little too much to drink, but some of them actually stayed just to pacify him and waited until I got there. I had to do a couple of counts with him and of course most of the people just wanted to get home after a long day. One woman came up to me and wanted to know how I trained him. I told her I couldn't reveal the secret. She then asked me if I trained dogs and would I train hers. I declined. After that ordeal, I changed my running pattern.

We had Sultan quite a few years and when he died, it

was like a member of the family dying. I can still remember Steven, LeeAnn, Carolyn and my nephew Richard Tobin (who lived with us at the time) all crying at the veterinarian's office.

Well, it wasn't long before we got another Golden (Monty). I tried teaching him the 'nod' . . . I guess he wasn't as smart because it didn't work.

Monty died a couple of years ago and Madeline had to get a cat; Molly is her name. I didn't try teaching her how to count, but the most amazing thing does happen with her. No one believes it, but it's true. As a frustrated singer, whenever I take a shower, I sing. Molly seems to know the scenario and patiently sits outside the shower meowing with me (we sound pretty good in this part of the house); she's the only one that actually enjoys my singing . . . must know talent when she hears it. I have also taught her to roll over and we will probably be going on the road soon if I can teach her any more tricks.

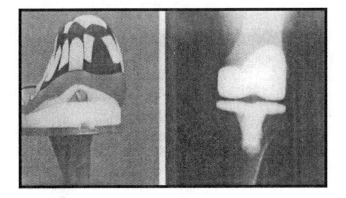

CHAPTER 23

TONY'S SCARS

I'VE PRETTY MUCH used up the information that I can remember, so I will be winding down pretty soon.

I do want to make you aware of another oddity with me. If you remember, I've stated how physically fit I was. Well, that's true; but it has come with a price. I could almost write a book in itself about my scars and call it "Tony's Scars"; so here it is from north to south.

I guess I was about thirteen or fourteen when this happened. I always liked to climb trees, especially this huge knurled oak on Wildwood Avenue, with Art Mulher, Ernie Aiello and Bob Tully. I think Carol Hellagas, one of the Wildwood gal tomboys, was also there. This tree was in the yard at the home of the family of movie actress Elaine Stewart, and was just up the street from where I lived.

I had almost reached the top when I slipped and fell through the branches onto the concrete, striking my head (maybe that's why I'm the way I am). I got about four stitches and my friends all swore they saw sawdust coming out from my head. Of course I don't know how they could see anything because they were laughing so hard they were rolling on the ground. Some friends—I could have been killed.

Going south, I have a large scar over my right eyebrow from running head-on into a tree in Brookdale Park, and the tree never budged. I was with Scott Bartlett at the time; two older guys, Artie Edelholf and Richard Schoenfield, were chasing us. When I looked back, I ran into the tree. I don't know where that tree came from and how come Scotty missed it? It wasn't there yesterday. I was about fifteen years old at the time.

I actually have another scar almost on top of that one. I got that while I was boxing at Charlie Johnson's house. He swears he hit me and knocked me into the post. But my story is I ducked his punch and, as I ducked, I hit the post. Either way I ended up with a few stitches and the scar.

Just south of my eyebrow is my nose. I banged it many times in football and boxing, apparently breaking it and not knowing it. I had just gotten out of the Navy and the doctor discovered I had a deviated septum, so when they operated on that they also had to straighten my nose, because I was told I was only getting fifty-percent breathing. Who knew? I ended up in St. Vincent's Hospital in Montclair for seven days.

Going further south, they discovered a large cyst by my left elbow. Fortunately it was not malignant, but it was removed with no problems.

We continue to go south to my kidney. Now this is a story.

I was getting stomach pains, so they put me in the hospital for observation. I was actually in there eight days. They couldn't find anything with my stomach but did find an infection in my kidney, and sent me to a kidney specialist. He immediately found a stone after looking at the x-rays. I asked this very serious doctor why hadn't the hospital found the stone while I was there for eight days having all those tests? He said the stone was about the size of a half-dollar but was apparently rolling around and that's probably why they missed it.

I very cleverly stated, "Do you mean to say I have one of the rolling stones?"

He looked at me very seriously and said, "Probably."

Well, I have a thirty-inch scar across my stomach because of a rolling stone (I tell my grandkids it's a zipper.)

I also have to add this about the kidney stone. I happened to be going to Montclair State College at the time. While I was in the hospital, I had to miss a couple of classes. There was one, however, I couldn't miss, and that was Doctor Coder's class for Drivers Education. I actually had to get a slip from the hospital to release me for that evening (eight PM to ten PM) to go to the class. Fortunately, it was only while I was having all the tests, before they found the "rolling stone."

While in the parking lot at the college, Dr. Coder singled me out, stating I had come from the hospital so I wouldn't miss the class. I had to raise my hand and show the hospital band to all the students. He then stated, "No one misses my classes. There is only one person off tonight. I gave him off because his wife passed away." He wasn't kidding. Dr. Coder was tough.

Well, to go further down my scar list would be my prostate. No, I didn't have it removed, but I had to have it shaved because it was slightly enlarged. That seemed to go pretty normal and it happened about ten years ago, so maybe I'm in the clear.

Well, right near the prostate is the colon. I don't know if that's north or south or where, but it's close by. No, I didn't have that removed either. But a few years earlier I had polyps and they were removed. This time, I believe it was 1993 and I again had polyps removed but one was found to be cancerous. I had to go back in and get all the tissue around the polyp removed. The doctor believed he had removed all the cancerous cells, so he didn't feel I would need any further treatment. The hospital wanted to put me on radiation but the doctor and I both agreed not to, so we left it as is. It's been ten years, so hopefully we were both right.

Now my right knee is the next scar. I have a ten-inch scar from having ripped my tendons many years ago right after I got out of the Navy. Jimmy Nasisi and I were wrestling down at the shore on the boardwalk of Seaside Heights, just fooling around; he landed on me, with my leg slipping from under me, ripping the tendons. I had an operation to have them retied.

My left knee was scoped in 1994 while I was working in the hospital. The doctor who performed that operation couldn't believe I came back to work so soon. He operated on me on a Thursday and I came back on a Monday. He said, "Tony, what are you doing here? You were supposed to go for therapy this week." I told him I did my own therapy Saturday and Sunday and it felt fine. He said, "Let me see you walk." I did and he said, "Great, just keep doing what you have been doing."

"Okay, Doc," I said, "but don't charge me for the therapy."

As I walked away I heard him tell another doctor nearby, "See, I just operated on him Thursday and he's walking already. Quite a job I did, huh?"

Well, the last scar—yep, you guessed it. It's as far south as you can go. My left toe. Many years ago, I had my toenail removed because of an ingrown toenail. I actually had to have it done twice because it grew in again. The doctor who removed it the second time said, "I can't believe this grew back again."

I said, "Believe it, Doc."

And you know what? I think I have to have it done a third time. Hey, I thought you stopped growing after age twenty-seven.

I did forget one. My right middle finger. I had three stitches from the turkey caper with my mother . . . remember that story?

I wish I was done with the scars but unfortunately, I don't think I am. My right knee has developed so much arthritis that it bothers me whenever I play a lot of games and do a lot of running. I'm all right if I just hit singles, but any more than that, it starts to bother me. The doctor already had told me about three years ago that I was a good candidate for a knee replacement, but he knows I want to continue playing ball so believes I wouldn't do it.

Actually, I am contemplating it because a couple guys I play with have had it done. One guy, Jerry Russo, runs faster than me. In fact, he runs faster than most all of the players, and he had his done over three years ago. There are numerous guys that I play with who need knee replacements. We're going to all go in at once; maybe they'll give us a cut rate.

I'm not done with this scar chapter because weeks have passed since I wrote that last statement, and I do have to have the knee replacement. It will be done in about one month, and hopefully I'll be able to play in the Olympics in June. If this book isn't complete by then, there will be an update on this scar chapter.

Well, here's the update:

As stated, I said I would add to this chapter if I got the knee replacement. Well, I had it done on March 19th—a very memorable day not only for me but also for all of the American people. On the same day they were cutting my knee out, the American forces invaded Iraq, eventually toppling Saddam Hussein's reign. As of this writing we still have troops stationed in the area with the hope of capturing Hussein.

I was in Morristown Memorial Hospital for three days for the operation, and then sent to Kessler Institute in West Orange for rehabilitation. This also was a very memorable time. I was amazed at how dedicated the physical therapists had been. I had Kirk and Polly and both were such dedicated people I couldn't believe it. It's amazing how we take the little things for granted, like dressing and tying your shoes. In the beginning it had to be done for me and I really couldn't start the day until I had help. I was very fortunate; I was in pretty good shape to start with so that was a big help. When I left there they told me I was a few weeks ahead of schedule and should have no problem as an outpatient, which I would have to be for a few weeks after I got home.

I have to tell you about this unbelievable story that occurred while I was in there. There was a gentleman eating right across from me who looked very familiar. I asked Don, a fellow I met who ate next to me, about him. He said, "Don't you know who that is? That's Bobby Thompson, the baseball player."

"Wow, are you kidding?" I said. "Do you think I could talk to him?"

"Sure," Don said, "he's very friendly."

For those of you who don't know who Bobby Thompson is, let me tell you. He's a Hall of Fame baseball player who played for the New York Giants when they were in New York in the 1950's. Those of you who know baseball know he's known for "the shot heard around the world." Let me explain that to you. On October 3, 1951, the Giants were playing the Dodgers at Ebbets Field. It was the last inning, there were two outs and the Giants were losing. Bobby Thompson came up with two men on base and hit a three-run homer, and the Giants won the game and the pennant. The announcer went crazy, yelling, "The Giants win the pennant, the Giants win the pennant!" Everyone else went crazy too, except Ralph Branca, the Dodger pitcher, and all the other Dodger fans.

So here was this big hero in front of me. I was such a Giants fan at the time I couldn't believe that here was the guy who changed everything that day with one swing of his bat, and I was about to talk to him. I humbly wheeled over to his wheel chair and said, "Hello, Mr. Thompson."

With a welcoming smile he said, "Please call me Bobby."

We talked for a short time and then I asked him about that historic home run: "the shot heard around the world," as everyone had referred to it, and he said, "Oh, that was no big thing."

Well, maybe to this very modest athlete it wasn't, but to all the Giants fans around the world—and this big Giants fan—it certainly was.

I talked with him for a while and told him I was still playing baseball and softball. We seemed to get along pretty well and I even asked him if he wanted to play on our team. He very politely refused, stating this last operation on his ankle ended his baseball playing days. I finally told him I was writing a book and gave him an excerpt for him to read. The next day he gave me the excerpt back and said he thought it was very good and would like to read the book. He even signed the excerpt for me and I asked him if I could put it in my book. And he agreed. I also promised him an autographed book (big deal). Imagine me offering a Hall of Famer an autographed book by this unknown average guy.

Well, meeting him made my stint at Kessler's much more memorable, and he certainly will get an autographed copy of the book from this excited fan.

CHAPTER 24

THOSE AMAZING BALL PLAYERS

EARLIER I HAD told you about the Senior Olympics, explaining to you about the games. Now I would like to tell you something about these amazing old athletes.

There are guys playing from all walks of life but we all have one thing in common: we all love the game of baseball. As I started talking to some of the guys I played with, I realized it would be very interesting to interview some of them and include them in my book, so I did that and here's what I found out.

Some of the guys who play are really unbelievable. One guy, Paul Oliver, is seventy-six and still going strong. He was an All-State football and baseball player out of St. Louis, Missouri. He played with Yogi Berra in the American Legion and lived on the same block as Yogi and Joe Garagiola. In fact, he did get a minor league contract and played in the minors with Stan Musial and Enos Slaughter for a short time. I was at a party for his seventy-fifth birthday and discovered what an amazing man he is. He still is quite a player and plays on a tournament team that travels all around the United States. He played in the Senior Olympics with the seventy-five-year-olds in June 2003 in Norfolk, Virginia, winning a silver medal.

I had mentioned Don Slocum earlier, and he plays like a forty-year-old. Not only is he a great physical specimen, he is almost a genius. He has his doctorate and has written numerous books and published many articles. He has had at least three patents and was the inventor of "Corian," the solid surface counter top material. I just found out from one of the players that the name Corian came from Don's daughter, Carol Ann. It seems his very young daughter couldn't say her name and it came out as "Corian."

Every time I talk to Don, I become more and more impressed. He also worked with Hoffmann-LaRoche as a chemist for many years and seems to know everything about vitamins. He acts as our "team doctor," always telling the guys what to do for the aches and pains they have. He constantly is going around the world consulting on different subjects. On top of all this, he is the one of the organizers getting the teams ready for the Olympics. He played and managed for the seventy-fives at Norfolk, Virginia in June 2003. Don has also initiated the seniors' hardball team and is a catcher on the team.

Don is about sharing, and recently I had the distinct honor of viewing a speech he made and his words jumped right off the page. I knew I had to share his creative and insightful vantage point with you. Don, you continually keep us ever young on our field of dreams, but you also keep us thinking. I now share your three positive "Slocum Precepts." Go, Don:

> First, remember your heritage. Not some ancestral aspect but the totality of your life experiences. Your family and friends, your

teachers and preachers, and all your history, as all these are a part of you. They belong to you and they are a source of strength.

Precept number two is: Take care of your body. Keep it healthy and fit because it is the vessel for your mind, your soul and your heart. And it is these that make up your character and that is certainly worth caring for. This will allow you to use your talents, putting them to work for the benefit of yourself and those around you. Creativity is nurtured by a healthy body and mind, and many times I needed to rely on endurance and stamina to give me strength on my journey to creative solutions.

The third and final precept is: You must believe! First in yourself, then in life, then in those values you cherish even now which as a youth sustained you in your quest that brought you to this pinnacle. And continue to believe. Even an inventor like Edison, or a theoretician like Fermi, or a Shakespeare, a Rembrandt, a Chopin, needed the confidence and surety of self to have accomplished what they did. I'm proud to say I've written many technical articles, I've been awarded numerous patents and introduced a number of commercial products. However, had I heeded the nay-sayers and listened to the skeptics, chances are I would have accomplished little along the way. So remember—never stop believing.

Well, Don, I didn't hear you give that commencement address, but your words made me feel like I was one of the new graduates. It's been an honor to know you and play ball with such an accomplished person. Even now, you continue to guide us as if we were today's youth, bringing out the best not just in me, but all of us "young oldsters," where the common denominator is "The Field Of Dreams." Thanks, Don Slocum.

Tommy Morris is another amazing guy. He played second base for us in the Olympics and although not a great hitter, always seems to get his hits. Probably the most amazing thing about Tommy is that he's even playing this year. Just before the season began, he had a heart attack and required a quadruple bypass. Within two months Tommy was playing again. He started slowly and is almost back to his original playing condition. He is a great organizer and was my assistant manager on my Tuesday team. He is also on the Softball Commissioners Board, setting up the rules and schedules for the leagues.

Bobby Pizutti is a retired Montclair Fire Chief, and the "Chief," as we call him, played and managed the sixty-fives in Baton Rouge, Louisiana in 2001. In June 2003 the Chief entered his own sixty-fives tournament team in the Olympics, representing New Jersey. His tournament team won it all in 2002. He plays first base and is quite a hitter. I had played against him for many years in the town leagues and of course the police-firemen games, and I had gotten him to play with us after he had retired from the Fire Department.

Carl (Nookie) Lombardi didn't play this year. He had injured his shoulder. He's seventy-six and was a great player. In high school he was an All-State football and baseball player. He even entered the Golden Gloves and won that also. He was some athlete. After high school he got a minor league baseball contract and played with the famous Mickey Mantle in Triple A ball. He's the one responsible for getting me to play in the seniors league. We had played in the town league together when he informed me about it. I had never even heard about it until he told me of it. Thanks, Nookie.

Harry Martin is an amazing man. At age seventy-eight, he's not a great ball player but shows up all the time and really gives it his all. And why wouldn't he? Harry Martin was and still is a real hero. Maybe not on the ball field, but in real life. He was an infantryman in the Second World War and fought in the famous "Battle of the Bulge," a fierce battle which many believe was the turning point in the defeat of the German Army. Harry was wounded in many parts of his body by shrapnel and ultimately received the Purple Heart and Bronze Star medals for his exploits. He has been writing a book on the events titled *I'm No Hero.* If you read the book, you will discover that the very modest Harry Martin was definitely a hero. Thousands of Germans and Americans lost their lives during this fierce battle, and Harry lived to tell this most amazing story. The book has not been published as yet but I'm sure some publisher will pick up this autobiography. This story must be told for all Americans to read this very important part of our history. Good luck, Harry—I am honored to be associated with you and playing ball with HARRY MARTIN—A REAL HERO.

I mentioned Walter Maly earlier, as manager and pitcher for "The Embers." He was instrumental in starting the team many years ago and had been pitching for them in the Olympics for many years. He has actually pitched a shut-out in the Olympics and believe me, that is very difficult to do in slow-pitch softball. Mary Ellen, his wife, never misses the Olympics, and I'm glad she never answered my note many years ago in high school, because they make a great couple.

Richard Palmer is another amazing player. Not only is he an excellent pitcher but he is one of our long-ball hitters. He has been playing many years and he also pitched a shut-out in the Olympics in Norfolk, Virginia, 2003. He is one of the main persons who started the league, having started with his own team and gradually getting other teams to formulate the Seniors league.

CHAPTER 25

THE FIFTIETH REUNION

THE YEAR 2000 marked the year of our fiftieth reunion. I graduated from Montclair High School in 1950. We have had a couple of reunions, but I think this is the most memorable.

First of all, it lasted three days. We had the dinner on Friday night at the Montclair Country Club in West Orange. We had a visit at Montclair High School on Saturday, then a wine and cheese Saturday night as well as some also had the football dinner. Then Sunday we had a brunch.

Our committee did a great job. It consisted of Nancy (Forshay) and Bill Blake, Betty (Kelleher) Ferdon, Dinne (Monte) Saunders, Mary Jane (Thompson) Erickson, Eugene Naspo, Donald Stake, Sandy Davis, Julie Stanisci and myself. Eleanor and Jack (Jake) Claren, who live in Colorado, helped us out via the computer. Everyone did a great job and it was a memorable experience.

We decided to have one every five years now because not only is our population dwindling, it's harder to see and hear each other as we get older. After all, at the next one we will all be seventy-three years old. Funny thing, none of the gals can lie about their ages, but I guess we could all say we're younger. No one would tell. Besides, at this age, who cares— we're just happy to be here.

Of course my wife said I again made a fool of myself by jumping on the table three times. I told her some of the people couldn't see too well, so that's why I repeated it. Next time we have it I said I can pretend to do it and could probably convince some of them that I did.

Let's hope I get this book out before the next reunion, which is now less than two years away.

CHAPTER 26

THE END

YOU KNOW I'VE never written a book before, so I really don't know how to end it. I know I've run out of most of my material that I can remember, so I may have to end it. The problem is I don't want to end it. Hey, I'm still here and things are still happening to me, so why should I?

Before I do, I do want to mention some people along the way who have really helped me.

Of course, there's my wife, Madeline, and although she hasn't actually put too much input in the book, she certainly has encouraged me. I guess it was like reverse psychology. She would get me so mad that I wanted to get away and just work on my book. So, "Thanks, honey. I know you have gotten pretty tired of me working on this thing and it's almost over. But you must remember I wouldn't be me if it were not for you. You have stuck with me all these years being a clown and never acting serious, and now that this is almost over maybe I can become more serious."

And of course my kids have had the same problem with me. In fact my son said to me recently, "Hey Dad, what do you want to be when you grow up?" Well, they must know that I am very serious about how I feel about all of them. They all know I love them very much and even though I clown around a lot, I have serious feelings for them.

Now I have to get a little serious and finish this up.

I would like to acknowledge Grange "Peggy" Rutan Habermann, a professional writer, a more-than-fifty-year friend who almost became my sister-in-law and even caught the bouquet at my wedding. Without her direction, I would never have completed this journey. Her inspirational writing abilities allowed me to tap into the latent author in me. She somewhat abandoned her own writings to help me and get me to the finish line.

Grange, I never would have come this far without your help. Of course Rolf, her husband, was solely responsible for "lending" her to me for the journey of my book and endured endless hours of editing. Thanks, Grange, and thank you, Rolf, my dear friends.

CHAPTER 27

THE REAL END

LET'S GET SERIOUS. As I realize, I have to end this journey, even though I don't want to leave you. My life flashes before me and I fully understand, above all, I have to thank God for allowing me to live through this ordeal which I have called "My Life." I have never been a very religious person but rest assured, I have done more than my share of praying throughout the years.

More than anything, I owe a lot of kudos to my lovely wife, Madeline, as she has never stopped believing in me, and because of her religious beliefs and my prayers I'm convinced this is truly the reason I survived.

Madeline, honey, you need to hear this, straight from the heart. This is for you:

How many nights did you watch me get into my uniform, strap on my weapon and leave, sometimes in the middle of the night, never knowing what was going to happen and even if I would be back? What were you thinking as you watched me leave? You must have been afraid, alone with the children in the house; in your own way you must have endured as much as I did and maybe even more. You certainly lived up to your part of the partnership and I hope I have lived up to mine.

I'm sure all policemen's and firemen's wives have endured the same anxieties. It never was really noticeable until 9/11 but we know it has always been there. Now a good part of the general public is also aware, tuned into the evil that lurks out there in the world.

And then of course there was my mother. She always thought I could do anything. She actually thought I was going to be a movie star. Sorry, Mom.

My father, even though he had quite a drinking problem, gave me incentive as I watched him toil at two jobs all his life so that we could have a better existence than he had. He taught me that good honest hard work is the way to get ahead and always believed in me and encouraged me. I followed his way of life, holding down two jobs most of my life. Actually, because of his drinking problem I chose not to drink. "Thanks, Pop."

And of course all my kids, Steven, LeeAnn and Carolyn, who were probably the biggest incentive to work hard and try to give them more than I have had. I hope that I have succeeded in doing that.

Steven, my only son, I am very proud to see what you have become. I see a lot of myself in you and hope that you will always remain the good family man that you have become, and pray for good health for all of you.

LeeAnn, my oldest daughter, I am very proud of how you have brought up your family and how you have continued to better yourself and your family by continuing your education and doing so well at it. Good health to all of you.

Carolyn, my baby girl: you'll always be my baby, even though you have your own beautiful baby boy, Davie. You have become quite a mother and I wish you good health to all your family.

Dad loves you all. And this book is for all of you.

And lastly I would like to thank all the good honest policemen all over the world who every day toil at a very difficult task that most people are not even aware of.

Really, this is the last statement of this book: "YOU'LL NEVER BELIEVE IT."

I'd like to know . . . do you believe it?

IT'S TRUE . . . HONEST.

BY: RETIRED LIEUTENANT ANTHONY NATURALE